Lifecraft

Also by Forrest Church

AUTHOR

Father and Son
The Devil and Dr. Church
Entertaining Angels
The Seven Deadly Virtues
Everyday Miracles
Our Chosen Faith
    (with John A. Buehrens)
God and Other Famous Liberals
Life Lines

EDITOR

Continuities and Discontinuities in Church History
    (with Timothy George)
The Essential Tillich
The Macmillan Book of Earliest Christian Prayers
    (with Terrence A. Mulry)
The Macmillan Book of Earliest Christian Hymns
    (with Terrence A. Mulry)
The Macmillan Book of Earliest Christian Meditations
    (with Terrence A. Mulry)
One Prayer at a Time
    (with Terrence A. Mulry)
The Jefferson Bible
    (with Jaroslav Pelikan)
Without Apology: Meditations by A. Powell Davies

Lifecraft

The Art of Meaning in the Everyday

Forrest Church

BEACON PRESS
BOSTON

Beacon Press
25 Beacon Street
Boston, Massachusetts 02108-2892
www.beacon.org

Beacon Press books
are published under the auspices of
the Unitarian Universalist Association of Congregations.

Printed in the United States of America

05 04 03 02 01 00   8 7 6 5 4 3 2 1

This book is printed on recycled acid-free paper that contains at least 20
percent postconsumer waste and meets the uncoated paper ANSI/NISO
specifications for permanence as revised in 1992.

Text design by Sara Eisenman
Composition by Wilsted & Taylor Publishing Services

Library of Congress Cataloging-in-Publication Data
Church, Forrest.
    Lifecraft : the art of meaning in the everyday / Forrest Church.
        p.   cm.
    ISBN 0-8070-7712-7 (alk. paper)
    1. Religious life.   2. Meaning (Philosophy)—Religious aspects.   I. Title.
  BL624.C495   2000
  248.4—dc21   99-057359

To John Williams and David Smith

The life so short, the craft so long to learn.
—Geoffrey Chaucer, 1381

Craft (kraft). *sb.* (Teutonic: OE. *craeft*). The original meaning is "strength, force, power, virtue." In English there is a transference from these original meanings to "skill, art, skilled occupation."
I. (originally): strength, power, might, force
II. Skill, art (*art* and *craft* were formerly synonymous)
   1. Ingenuity in constructing, dexterity
   2. Occult art, magic
   3. Human skill, art as opposed to nature
   4. A skillful contrivance or artifice
   5. A spell, or enchantment
   6. Deceit, guile, fraud, cunning
III. The learning of the schools, scholarship
IV. A branch of skilled work
V. Applied to boats, ships, and fishing vessels
VI. *-craft* is also the second element in many compounds, for example, handicraft, kingcraft, priestcraft, statecraft, watercraft, witchcraft, and so on.

(as in)

Lifecraft
I. Human strength, power, might, creative force, virtue
II. The art of being, the discovery and creation of meaning
   1. Creation
   2. Divinization
   3. Spirituality, also good works
   4. Idolatry
   5. Mystification
   6. Blasphemy
III. Wisdom
IV. The art of meaning
V. A vessel or conveyance that takes us toward life's meaning, often in search of God

Contents

Preface   xi

Introduction   3

1: Pictures from an Exhibition   13

2: Self-Portraits   25

3: Character and Plot   37

4: Tombs and Monuments   53

5: The God Project   67

6: The Music of Prayer   81

7: A Mystery Story   95

8: Poetry in Motion   107

Afterword   119

Preface

Let me begin by telling you a little about yourself. To one extent or another the following is true:

You are self-conscious about your appearance.
You feel guilty about things you have done or failed to do.
You sometimes have a hard time accepting yourself or forgiving others.
You are insecure sexually.
You are a less-than-perfect parent, or a less-than-perfect child of imperfect parents, or both.
You are a frustrated husband, wife, or partner, or you are frustrated not to be a husband, wife, or partner.
You have secrets, which you might betray, or which might betray you, at any moment.
However successful you are, you fail in ways that matter both to you and to your loved ones.
Beyond all this, your life is stressful, your happiness fleeting, your health insecure.
You worry about aging.

You sometimes worry about dying.

More than once your heart has been broken by betrayal or loss.

And however successful you may be, however deep your faith,
  when the roof caves in, you shake your fist at heaven, the fates, or
  life itself.

You beg for an answer to the question "Why?"—"Why this? Why
  me? Why now?"

You wonder what your life means.

  All of the above holds true for me as well. Not that I don't have my
own quirks. Among other things,

I have dealt with lust by taking off my glasses.

I read two tabloids almost every day.

I have lied to my parents and also to my children.

I have lied to my wife when I didn't even have to.

I have done things that shouldn't make me feel bad about myself
  but do just the same.

When I succeed, I worry about my failures.

When I fail, I worry about my success.

I have quenched my fears sometimes with drink and sometimes
  with anger.

I do everything I can to avoid pain.

And yet I am loved so deeply that all I fear should be washed away
  by love's tide.

  So what do I have to teach? First, this. After a quarter century
of pastoral counseling and twice that of personal failures and
successes, I have learned that we are what we love. If we love too
deeply something too small for so deep an attachment, our love will
destroy both it and us. If we love only in little ways, even if the

object is as big as God, our love will be insufficient. Any quest for meaning searches the human heart. I am more wary about our minds. Knowledge may be virtue, as Socrates once said, but he also boasted that he was the most ignorant man in Athens. Knowing more than anyone, he recognized how little he actually knew.

Decidedly less knowledgeable than Socrates, I am nonetheless ignorant enough to know a little about the art of meaning. To begin with, meaning is not absolute; no suit fits all. To witness the complete destruction of meaning, ponder the wreckage when a terrorist possessed by Truth delivers a plane full of innocent passengers to his "God." Neither is meaning relative. The logic of relativism blurs distinctions and neutralizes judgment, reducing life to a shambles. Finally, meaning is contextual. When lost in self-absorption, my life may churn, but it means very little. As the Reverend William Sloane Coffin puts it, "There is no smaller package in the world than someone who is all wrapped up in himself."

In the pages to follow, I invite you to unwrap yourself. First, open your mind. People with closed minds fail to recognize that we are more alike in our ignorance than different in our knowledge. And then open your heart. Meaning can be found almost anywhere, but the meanings that matter most always spring from love.

Before I begin, let me make a few acknowledgments. As always, I thank my parishioners, the congregation of All Souls in New York City, for their insight, courage, steadfastness, and support. My wife, Carolyn Buck Luce, and children, Frank, Nina, Jacob, and Nathan, also teach me, every single day, more than I am able to learn.

Among the many others who helped me bring this book to final form, I am especially indebted to Khoren Arisian, Nancy King Bernstein, Theodore Bikel, David Black, Julie Brannon, Richard Cashin, Bill Coffin, Alison Collins, Bill Grimbol, Annie Gorycki,

Preface

Galen Guengerich, Alison Miller, Christopher Hayden, Mary-Ella
Holst, Dana Ivey, Richard Leonard, Wayne Rood, all the great people from Beacon Press, Helene Atwan, Micah Kleit, Deanne Urmy,
and Mary Ray Worley, and, of course, my mother, Bethine (you
must always thank your mother). None is responsible for anything
wrong here, but all deserve credit for much that turned out right.

I dedicate this book to the political economist John Williams of
Melbourne University, as humble a brilliant man as I have known.
I met John during a month's stay in Australia when I was visiting
preacher for Saint Michael's Church in Melbourne. A dedicated
Libertarian, John inspires me to articulate my religious views
(which we share) and political ones (which we don't) more persua-
sively than I otherwise might. For his many contributions to *Lifecraft,* I thank him, confident that—splendid sparring partner that
he is—he will gently point out ways I could have made it better.

I also dedicate this book to a dear man in my congregation, David
Smith, a fabulously successful doctor and scientist (he both discovered and created a prevention for spinal meningitis). On reading *Life Lines,* my last book, David dared me to be a little more
spiritual here. I have certainly tried. When dying of cancer, by
employing meditation, prayer, and a thousand acts of kindness, he
far outlived everyone's expectations. To the day of his death, for his
wife, Joan, his daughters, and so many others, David proved that
life has meaning.

New York City, January 2000

Lifecraft

Introduction

The search for meaning is a religious search. Admittedly, I define religion broadly. I don't restrict the religious impulse to those who identify with the rules and beliefs of distinct communities of faith. Putting aside the existence or nonexistence of God—even Buddhists don't "believe" in God—my definition of religion is simple and inclusive: *Religion is our human response to the dual reality of being alive and having to die.* Knowing that we are going to die, we question what life means. We are not so much the animal with advanced language or the animal with tools as we are the religious animal. Having discovered relics and flowers in ancient graves, certain anthropologists actually apply to us the sobriquet *homo religiosus.* We have honored our dead from time immemorial, even as we continue to sift through their ashes in anticipation of our own earthly remains.

If you define religion more narrowly (as a group whose rites and practices involve belief in and worship of God), my point still holds. From atheist to Christian, we mortals are seekers of meaning. In response to the dual reality of being alive and having to die, we question what life means while attempting to create meaning within it. To answer this question, what an abundance of material

[3]

we have to shape and ponder. Our lives are novels, filled with diverse characters and shifting plots, narratives connected and configured by memory. Our lives are pictures from an exhibition, snapshots in an album. They are molded and remolded from human clay. They are carved and weathered, built and remodeled. With a given melody and added harmonies, our lives, whether marked more by consonance or dissonance, can compose themselves into majestic symphonies. I call this—the art of meaning—lifecraft.

Lifecraft can be practiced on a canvas or in the office, in a relationship or by the bedside of a loved one who is dying. In the bad sense of craft, it also takes shape through subterfuge. There is good art and bad art, good meaning and bad. We practice the art of meaning, well or poorly, in a million ways throughout our lives. In a twisted form (and every good thing can be twisted), lifecraft entails craftiness and deception as well as good works and God-seeking. With only a nod to the former, I shall focus here on lifecraft in its positive sense. Think of lifecraft as a power that we possess and can choose to exercise, or as the art by which we discover and create meaning. Go even further. Think of your lifecraft as a vessel sailing in the direction of God.

With a little training and perseverance, anyone can practice lifecraft. We're not talking great art here, only useful art. Begin by thinking of pot holders and throw rugs, key chains and quilts, and then expand the metaphor. In the 1970s, Oxford philosopher Bernard Williams suggested the model I shall follow by theorizing about the nature of personal identity in terms of projects.

Imagine your life as a series of works in progress presented daily at a craft fair. Each day's exhibits present an overlapping series of projects—the child project, the parent project, the love project, the vocation project, the justice project, even the God project. Add and subtract community projects and recreation projects, house projects and old friend reclamation projects. You might work on a project to enhance your church or college or to improve your neighborhood. Less important projects also possess meaning, like attempts to lose weight or to improve your health. Another long-term project might be to read all of Edward Gibbon's *History of the Decline and Fall of the Roman Empire* or Marcel Proust's *Remembrance of Things Past*. We work on dozens of projects at once, tasks that invest our lives with meaning.

Through hard work on even a single project, we may discover meaning. At the same time, we can also create meaning. Something that otherwise couldn't have existed emerges from our effort. We don't just "have" ideas. Most ideas emerge at intersections in our lives. They occur when we see, do, hear, or feel something overlaid on something else. It is magic when this happens. Yet we rarely do this alone. Someone gives us the lines, and we color them in. Or we give them the lines, and they add the color. It doesn't really matter. We discover and create something that did not exist before. By taste and according to circumstance, the colors differ. So do the lines. That is why meaning is not absolute. There are millions of ways to do almost anything. Yet meaning is not purely relative either. The meanings we discover and create can be judged by their impact on other people's lives.

When you make another person feel safe or loved, you create meaning. When you accomplish a difficult project, you also create meaning. Of the two—enhancing the security of others or completing an important task—neither is inherently more meaningful. This century's most brilliant scientist, Albert Einstein, didn't necessarily have a more meaningful life than anyone who can honestly claim to have married well. The same caution holds in other arenas of human accomplishment. Just before he died, after five failures, J. Paul Getty said that he would trade his entire fortune for a single happy marriage. Fortunately, for most of us the choice is not between one thing (discovering the theory of relativity, making a fortune) or another (having a happy marriage). The marriage project itself breaks down into smaller, more manageable projects. By doing a single thing to make our spouse happier and by sustaining it over time, we can change the entire dynamic of a marriage. The same holds for other relationships, in fact for any of life's problems. If we break down problems into projects—to borrow an image from one of my parishioners—it's usually not one big gorilla on your back (although it sometimes it feels like one). It's more likely to be a bunch of little monkeys that you can pick off one at a time.

Our spiritual search—the God project if you will—can be viewed in a similar light. Instead of positing and searching for one great truth that imbues all life with meaning, we can add up little truths one by one. This is not the usual practice in theology. On the contrary, most theologians tackle life's meaning as they might a Rubik's Cube, a puzzle with a single solution. Let me take this little toy to illustrate the difference between my approach and theirs.

My All Souls ministerial colleague Richard Leonard has what may be the world's largest collection of Rubik's Cubes. Among his two hundred cubes are not only the familiar six-color cube that most of us have seen (and been frustrated by) but also far more difficult cubes with pictures on each side. Dick has a cube from Prince Charles and Princess Diana's wedding, Christmas cubes, and Hanukkah cubes, even slightly racy cubes. If you've seen it, he probably has one.

Those who know what they are doing can solve the six-color cubes in three minutes flat with about one hundred turns, every turn correct. I asked Dick how many incorrect combinations were possible. The answer is staggering: more than 43 quintillion (43,252,003,274,489,855,999 exactly). Even before they had a working model, imagining a like cube, Greek mathematicians arrived at this very number two and a half millennia ago, a solution that has been ratified by number theorists to this very day.

Compared to life itself, a Rubik's Cube seems relatively uncomplex. Yet, to get a sense of how many possible configurations are on this little toy, compute the number of seconds in a 13 billion–year universe (the formula is $60 \times 60 \times 24 \times 366 \times 13{,}000{,}000{,}000$). The result is one hundredth of the number of potential Rubik's Cube permutations. Randomly twisting a Rubik's Cube once a second, you would spend fifty universe lifetimes before the odds turned in your favor for accidentally solving the puzzle. It is humbling (and also awesome) to consider that our lives admit exponentially more combinations than do Rubik's Cubes.

To answer the riddle of human existence, most theologians treat the meaning of life exactly as they might a Rubik's Cube. "God sent his only son, Jesus, to die for our sins, in order that those of us who believe that he is Lord and Savior may be baptized in his blood and go to heaven when we die" is one such answer to the question "What does life mean?" I do my best to follow Jesus' teachings, and sometimes (on my good days) I call myself a Christian, but given the manifold possibilities for discovering and creating meaning, I cannot embrace a dogmatic creed, even one established in Jesus' name.

For me, our lives are more like interactive mosaics or stained glass windows, some pieces or panes set at birth, some placed by effort, others shifting according to happenstance. We are each a pastiche of works, our lives ever under construction and development. Though recognizable from the beginning, they take shape as we grow, love, fail, and recover. They change as we develop, and as the world changes us. We comprise multiple surfaces of fixed and movable, interchangeable images that together compose and recompose our lives. On any given day, some pieces are broken, some miscolored or badly cast. Others are fixed intractably in place. At least as many move, and every move offers an opportunity for new hope and insight. Remember, there are infinitely more than 43 quintillion variations. Myriads of these present to the searching eye a window on beauty, truth, and love.

To shift the metaphor a bit, we each look out our window at the world, but through one set of panes at a time. As children, parents, spouses, bosses, employees, and friends, we are different people in differing contexts. We look upon and are viewed by our world in many ways. Even as a fifty-year-old adult, I am a child, and sometimes childish, when speaking to my mother. Beyond this, I am a preacher, pastor, lover, social activist, baseball fan, country music aficionado, writer, father, husband—the list (including things I am too proud to mention) goes on and on. D. H. Lawrence said that each of us, as long as we remain alive, is in him- or herself a multitude of conflicting people. This rings true to me. In some contexts I am shy, even insecure, in others affable and outgoing. Even within a given context, playing a familiar role, I can be a different person according to shifting mood or backdrops that color the same setting in a brighter or more forbidding light. Since by nature and nurture we are cast in many roles and evince multiple personae, our search for an authentic self (the essence of our being) is no less vain than is our quest for ultimate meaning.

Fortunately, life is not a puzzle to be solved but a series of projects to accomplish as best we can. It is not a work in progress but a series of works in progress. Lifecraft embraces living and dying, loving and losing, failing well, recovering, and coping. The light of meaning refracts through many filters, some rosy, some dark, each changing the light behind them. From this perspective, life becomes meaningless only when we look selectively through the darkest panes of our window, the panes that block the light.

For instance, if we view our lives not in terms of projects or in parts but as a whole, when we fail in a single project—our job, health, a relationship—we may view life's meaning through only one beclouded lens and quickly become despairing. As long as we think of ourselves in absolute terms as successful or unsuccessful, healthy or ill, victor or victim, saved or damned, the moment the world turns against us, as surely it will, we risk sacrificing all sense of meaning.

There is never a time when something in our lives could not, in and of itself, trigger a sense of meaninglessness or hopelessness. If we are struggling with but a single important aspect of our lives, even the sun sometimes seems cruel. When I get anxious or depressed, as I do from time to time, it is usually because I am focusing on a single part of my life that has gone awry. This puts me in blinders; I lose my peripheral vision. Even little things can throw me out of kilter. Blocking out the good, I see only the bad in myself or my situation. While writing this book, I was sometimes anxious and depressed the very same day! But then another project saved me. On several occasions it was a comfort the dying and their families project, through which the light of new meaning parted the shadows of my self-absorption. I have seen people on their death-beds take the final note of life and turn it into a symphony. To be present at such a moment is to hear the angels sing.

It begins with a phone call, followed by a few pastoral encounters, often a crisis, sometimes a deathbed confession. Or just holding hands with another human being, mysteriously born, fated to die, who is about to find out what happens next, which neither of us really knows. Here meaning is completely contextual. We throw parent and child projects and fighting for life and accepting death projects into the mix. We rise (or fall) to the occasion, with tears, often a remarkable amount of laughter, almost always great regret and sadness, ideally humility, sometimes humiliation as the body falls apart, and then, good-bye. This too is lifecraft, perhaps even the boat that takes us back to God.

Some people resolve the contradictions that might render life meaningless by positing a next life in which scores will be settled. We know that good people get bad breaks and bad people good ones. A theology of the afterlife satisfies our need for fairness. In heaven, the good receive compensation for unfair hardship; in hell, the bad endure damnation for their earthly triumphs and unpunished sins. Driven by the logic of justice, this is nonetheless a form of magical or wishful thinking. We know infinitely less about what happens after we die than about what happens before. If we do live on after death, it wouldn't surprise me in the least. To live forever could be no stranger than to be born in the first place. But to draw from an experience we have not had (afterlife) in order to divine meaning from what we do experience (life) is, to cite the philosopher Alfred North Whitehead, an instance of misplaced concreteness.

Putting the question of an afterlife aside, because a loved one dies is life a sham? Astronomers tell us that our sun too will die. It will implode and then explode. When this happens, billions of years from now, the earth will be incinerated, its earthly remains spun into the cosmos. From a blade of grass to the earth itself, everything returns to dust. Is life thus rendered meaningless?

Existential philosopher Albert Camus asked himself daily whether he should choose to continue to live. I once was moved by this; now I find it silly. For me, the question is not "Whether?" but "How?" Having witnessed courage, repentance, even family redemption, at times of greatest trial, I chafe at those who trade in absurdity. The meaning we glean from life is written not with the final period but in between the lines. Meaning stems from how we meet life's exigencies, not from why things like pain and suffering exist. Pain and suffering can even be put to use. As Herman Melville said, "mishaps are like knives." They either serve us or cut us, depending on whether we grasp them by the blade or by the handle. Handling life well, whenever we surprise others and ourselves by rising to difficult occasions, we can redeem the darkest day. A stubborn man finally says he's sorry. A frightened soon-to-be widow tells her husband to let go, kisses him, and gently suggests that it is all right for him to leave her now. Meaning illuminates the darkness as well as the light.

More an art than a science or philosophy, in the practice of lifecraft meaning springs from very basic things. It emerges when a father works with his son on his homework night after night. Or when a woman fixes her energy on a project that makes her company, neighborhood, or family a little better. You may glimpse it when a couple invests their hard-earned money in a cause they believe in, becoming part of something greater and more lasting. Even, perhaps, when a beachcomber, like the naturalist Loren Eiseley, finds a starfish on the shore and throws it back into the sea.

Over the course of our lifetime, we paint, weave, cast and draw, design, and build our lives in ways that can, not always but often, lead us to find meaning within them. But lifecraft has a broader dimension as well. In our darkest moments, often in our finest, we can launch our little boat into the heavenly waters in search for God.

When someone tells me that she doesn't believe in God, I ask her a little about the God she doesn't believe in, because I probably don't believe in him either. Torching an idol is no more difficult, nor any less conducive to meaning, than bowing down before one. In his book *Ye Shall Be as Gods,* Erich Fromm wrote, "The approach to the understanding of what an idol is begins with the understanding of what 'God' is not. God is not man, the State, an institution, nature, power, possession, sexual powers, or any arti-fact made by man. . . . The idol is lifeless; God is living. The con-tradiction between idolatry and the recognition of God is, in the last analysis, that between the love of death and the love of life." A humanist penned these words, but they serve my theology well. By my definition, *God is not God's name. God is our name for that which is greater than all and yet present in each—the life force, ground of our being, being itself.*

In our encounters with others, but also with nature and art, we experience moments of peace and wholeness that reflect more elo-quently than any theology the underlying basis of our relationship to the ground of our being. Since God is beyond knowing or nam-ing—in our accustomed ways of seeing, both too close and too far away for us to see—we are most likely to discover God when our minds follow our hearts. If God is love—as good a metaphor as any—how we love is a better measure for God than anything we think or believe. This doesn't mean that God is actually love, only that love is divine.

When I think about God, I am testing my ability to hope, love, and find meaning. I shall fail in my search for God, but all of us fail. The key is to fail gracefully in a quest that truly matters, and in such a way that others feel better about their own failures. The secret is to return from this quest blessed with new eyes to glimpse the divine amid the ordinary and new ears to hear the still, small voice. Then sight becomes miracle, and hearing too.

No further proof is necessary.

1. Pictures from an Exhibition

We live in all we seek. The hidden shows up in too-
plain sight. It lives captive on the face of the obvious—
the people, events, and things of the day—to which we
as sophisticated children, have long since become
oblivious. What a hideout: Holiness lies spread and
borne over the surface of time and stuff like color.
—*Annie Dillard,* FOR THE TIME BEING

Surely, as we are simple men who
pose questions without answer,
we must be unceasing, stretch
what remains of canvas upon frame.
Granting to imagination its due.
Apply paint and hope for life revealed.
—*Daniel Moran, "In Praise of August"*

Jean Anouilh writes that "the object of art is to give life a shape."
This epitomizes lifecraft. Meaning emerges as a composition
might, a lifework on canvas or a musical score. First we sketch, then
augment and reconfigure our life notes into studies, etudes, that
express what we think, how we feel, who we are. As with the oeuvre
of great artists, we don't accomplish this in a single brush stroke or
composition, but through a series of lifeworks that illuminate one
another.

Our lives are like pictures from an exhibition, a special kind
of exhibition. We are both subject and viewer, as when we leaf
through old family photograph albums. There I am on my first

[13]

birthday, looking mysteriously like my own son, my father like me. Then, a little later, Forrest Church, five years old, crew cut, big ears, Harvard T-shirt, proudly holds up a pint-sized trout that should have been thrown back. Who is that little boy? He is I, and yet not I. Not only has much happened since to shape and change who I am, but much that happened before, constituting my five-year-old memories and dreams, is all but forgotten. There I am in one picture with my father's father, whom I obviously knew well but now do not remember. We are laughing together. It is a reminder that I too shall be forgotten.

In our family pictures, we are both viewer and subject, and not just one subject, but rather a series of subjects, familiar strangers, growing, changing, negotiating rites of passage, entering and passing through new stages of life. Not only do we change over age and time, but also we are known through our relationships. We play differing roles, both in the ways we behave and in the nature of our intimacies, attitudes, and personalities.

Think of the stunning Picasso retrospective that showed at New York's Museum of Modern Art in the late 1980s. On view were Picasso's pictures at an exhibition, paintings of life and from his life's experience, running from his early representational work through cubism, and on to the most evocative forms of abstract art. They compose a story in stages, of passages and changes. We feel Picasso's imprint on every canvas, and yet how different they are one from another. There are differences of mood within periods and between them. On his canvases are wars and rumors of war, evidences of pain deeply felt, his own and that of others. There is tragedy and compassion, but joy as well, and ample testimony to love, given and received, taken and betrayed. As Picasso himself once said, "Painting isn't an aesthetic operation; it's a form of magic designed as a mediator between this strange hostile world and us,

a way of seizing the power by giving form to our terrors as well as
our desires."

The ancient Gnostics believed that we have power over those
forces or demigods who would destroy us, but only if we know
their names. Picasso seized power, or wrested meaning, from the
world by giving form to his terrors and desires. He named them
on canvas and through sculpture. In his lifelong struggle for self-
expression, medium and method changed many times. But as a constant, Picasso himself remained fully engaged, alive, and growing
until the day of his death. Did he discover meaning and then give
it form, or by giving form to his terrors and desires did he create
meaning, or neither, or both?

The answer is "Both." If our lives have meaning—or, better, meanings—we both discover them and create them. To the extent that we
do neither, our lives may indeed be meaningless. This is not true
for most of us. Through a process of discovery and creation (with
certain projects short-lived and others works of a lifetime), meanings emerge, taking shape over time, developing according to
experience.

Much like Picasso's oeuvre, our lives, too, fluctuate from rose
to blue. They are representational for a time and then abstract.
Sometimes they scream from the canvas; other times they blend
harmoniously into their own landscape. Cardinal Newman once
said, "Here below to live is to change, and to be perfect is to have
changed often." By such a definition, Picasso's art—if not his life—
is as close to perfection as it can be, daring each of us to liberate
ourselves from the life-denying strictures of fear and rigidity. We
should not accept all dares, but when we cease daring to grow and
risking the changes growth will surely bring, not only is life's animating spirit stifled, but opportunities for the creation and discovery of meaning are suppressed.

[15]

Great artists explore the human situation not to dissect it but to present it whole, as it is lived, without fear or favor, without concealment or exaggeration. They help define the art of meaning. Think of Shakespeare. Procrastination surely has not been the same since *Hamlet,* jealousy since *Othello,* or opportunistic ambition since *Macbeth.* Nor, for that matter, have sunsets been the same since Turner, or the entire choir of heaven and of earth since Bach and Beethoven. Those who have seen furthest (and most dispassionately, for great art suspends judgment) have brought back from the deeper and less accessible layers of consciousness what is going on all the time beneath the surface in each of our lives. In studying their contributions to life's meaning, we anticipate the decisive and dangerous moments of experience and are more or less ready when they come, not only with the comprehensiveness of thought and the promptness of action but also with the inwardness of appropriate feeling.

Another set of pictures that illuminates the art of meaning is a piece of music written by the Russian composer Modest Mussorgsky (1839–81), in which a troubadour leads us through a gallery and describes, one by one, the paintings there. Mussorgsky's inspiration was the death of one of his closest friends, the artist Victor Hartmann. As a tribute, he chose to set his friend's art to music. Mussorgsky composed *Pictures from an Exhibition* for solo piano. Subsequently, it has been scored at least five times for full orchestra. The best-known transcriptions are those of Ravel and Stokowski. In the former, the voice of Mussorgsky's troubadour is written for an alto saxophone, in the latter for an English horn.

Each version might be seen as the original child come of age. In either case, the simplicity of the original is lost with full orchestration. Ravel added layers of complexity, whereas Stokowski's render-

ing, to me at least, rings untrue to its promise. It is brassy and
inauthentic. The same piece of music is recognizable in either case,
but of such different quality.

This recalls the argument of nature versus nurture. Which is the
principal instrument of our development? "Nature" proposes that
we are limited and determined by accidents of birth. We are born
with certain genetic, or to follow my example, thematic lines. We
cannot change the essence of who we are. "Nurture" responds that
others, particularly parents, teachers, friends, and colleagues,
orchestrate our development. Also, by purposive action, we create
who we will become. In balance, both arguments have merit and
correct one another. Novelist James Baldwin rightly says that "we
take our shape, it is true, within and against that cage of reality
bequeathed us at our birth, and yet is precisely through our dependence on this reality that we are most endlessly betrayed."

Even as each child enters the world as an original composition
with a given nature—with a set, as it were, of themes and melo-
dies—others shape and change us, adding harmonies and dissonance. We also shape and change (or orchestrate) ourselves.
Mussorgsky discovered something in his friend's paintings and created a new language by which to express that discovery. Ravel, Stokowski, and others then discovered in Mussorgsky's masterpiece a
subtext for their own creations. In our own lives, we discover the
meaning that is given. That which emerges from our actions, or
"projects," we help create.

Even as every flutter of a butterfly's wing or fall of a sparrow
slightly, if imperceptibly, changes nature, in the art of meaning our
every thought or action, if ever so slightly, changes the world.
Changes are not always for the better. Destructive endeavors can
shatter life's meaning, our own and, directly or accidentally, that of

[17]

others. An abusive husband or drunk driver can destroy life. Less dramatically, unsustained projects reduce our life's meaning to a chaotic shambles.

On the other hand, constructive projects we sustain give coherence to our lives, and in turn evoke meaning from them. As with Stokowski's and Ravel's orchestration of Mussorgsky, when others and we orchestrate our innate tune, our lives become complex or simply complicated, complete or overwrought. This is the challenge, burden, and promise of freedom.

Pictures from an Exhibition sheds light on our quest for meaning in an another sense. Mussorgsky selected sketches and portraits that run the gamut from birth (the ballet of unhatched chicks) to death (the catacombs), from imperfect innocence (children arguing at play) to thwarted love (a knight's plaintive appeal to his distant lady), from injustice (a rich man rejecting a poor man's appeal) to life's daily tasks and burdens (women gossiping in a marketplace and, poignantly, workers laboring in a field). In its original form, Mussorgsky's *Pictures from an Exhibition* is itself a search for meaning: what his dead friend's and his own life mean, what the world we live in means, how we can reconcile evil and God. As for the third of these triptychs, leading us from evil as a reality to redemption as a possibility (magically evoked by the music), the final two pieces do this brilliantly. First, the Russian witch Baba Yar makes a threatening appearance, and then the exhibition ends with a stirring tribute to the artist's proposed design for a grand gateway to Kiev. On Mussorgsky's musical canvas, life is painful, sometimes grotesque, suddenly beautiful, often filled with struggle, and, potentially, redemptive. Describing his own art as "not an end in itself, but a means of addressing humanity," he later added this caveat: "the boundaries of art in the religion of an artist mean stagnation."

[18]

By breaking down the boundaries between painting and music, Mussorgsky defied stagnation. In *Pictures from an Exhibition* he explored lost love, the burden of heavy labor, the reality of injustice, the superficiality of much human interaction, the presence and persistence of evil, even the democracy of death. Yet, after wandering through this gallery, first as a spectator and then (the music makes this clear) as a participant in the dramas he was pondering, Mussorgsky composed his thoughts into a rousing moral affirmation.

Mussorgsky's *Pictures from an Exhibition* represents one man's search as unveiled through a work of art, but in each of our lives the art of meaning finds expression in like ways. We ponder life's great questions, drawing insight from those who have preceded us. We color their experiences with our brush. We change mediums constantly and inspire others to shape their own reflections in combination with ours.

Reflecting on a single aspect of our own life or the life we share, sometimes we despair. But by sustaining our search through dark passages, and by collaborating on meaningful projects, aspects of the Hartmann/Mussorgsky model emerge in our own lifecraft. Although constituting a partial and limited model for the art of meaning, the creative processes leading up to Mussorgsky's masterpiece and following its completion indicate how lifecraft works.

Life's meaning has public as well as private dimensions. In our search for meaning we must contemplate, as did Mussorgsky, pictures of poverty and injustice, forlorn love, human vanity, evil, and death. Investing lifecraft with a moral dimension demands engagement with the world, its melancholy and even its tragedy. Failing to do this, the moment tragedy visits we will be unprepared to view our own lives in a larger context. Without a broad perspective on life's potential beauty and abiding squalor, the fragile meanings that bubble up out of the privacy of our self-absorption may turn to vapor.

Here Mussorgsky presents a splendid model, not for a happy life (he was a very troubled man) but in the ways he wrested meaning from his setbacks and losses. Inspired by his friend's imaginative vision, and through his own artistic endeavors, he found ways to affirm life over death, order over chaos, beauty over meaninglessness. His final affirmation is a triumph. For succeeding generations of seekers, Mussorgsky let the bells ring.

Even as Ravel and Stokowski shaped the same piece of music in such different ways, our existential freedom to move within and fill out the limits of our essential being is both exhilarating and chastening. When we refuse to shape our oeuvre or arrange our galleries by retaining what is good and abating what is bad, we diminish our own and others' lives by failing to discover and create meaning in them.

Each of us is the curator of his or her life. In our galleries of meaning, certain displays may be chaotic at times, but meaning emerges by the very act of trying to arrange our treasures, even by accepting what cannot be rearranged. More important than the final result is our willingness to work at our lives in the same way a curator might work on his or her collection, keeping the storage rooms in order, rehanging this gallery or that. As curators we are also artists. We can paint new canvases and restore old ones, as well as mounting and displaying them. Setting priorities and holding to them is more important even than the matériel given us to shape or the talent we are born with. There are limits to life itself, but no expiration date on making or finding meaning within it. For the things that matter most—the parent project, the child project, the partner, friend, and God projects—the only limit lies in our willingness to take such projects seriously. When instead we neglect them, reacting helter-skelter to every little demand life imposes, we squander the most important gift we are given both as artists and as curators of meaning, the gift of time.

I'm seldom impressed when people tell me they are busy. "Busy" people are less likely to be engaged in meaningful work than trapped in a cycle of frenetic futility, like flies trying to get out through a closed window. If we put off things that really matter or, as some people are fond of saying, wait to do the things we know we should be doing until we "get our life back," we will never get our life back. We'll never even "get a life."

Think of meaning in terms of project management. If our life is living us rather than our living it, we cede our project management to others. Rather than making the most of what we have, we fritter it away in starts and stops. Some life projects are prone to interruption by definition, the parent project, for instance. But even here we can work to balance long-term goals with short-term demands. A meaningful parenthood is proactive as well as reactive. Most of us expend roughly the same amount of energy parenting our children whether we do this mindfully or not, but the contrasting results will be pronounced. Good project management requires parallax vision. Even while flitting from task to task, or responding to unavoidable little demands, meaning can emerge from but a few moments of simultaneous reflection on the larger importance of the matter at hand.

Try this experiment. You are tending your children. Imagine for just a moment that a trapdoor swings. You or one of your loved ones drops out of the picture. The backdrop of our lives at any given instant may seem mundane or chaotic, but the bond between ourselves and our loved ones in the foreground is both unimaginably precious and very fragile. One day either you or they will be left with nothing but memories. A little nostalgia for the present

[21]

prevents such memories from becoming reflections on lost time, lost meaning, and lost love.

Thornton Wilder gives voice to this in his play *Our Town,* which focuses on the burial of Emily Webb, who has died in childbirth during her twenty-sixth year. In the cemetery, she recognizes friends and relatives who have died before her and discovers that one can return to the land of the living to visit one's past. They advise her not to hazard this, but Emily can't resist. The day she chooses to revisit is her twelfth birthday.

STAGE MANAGER: We'll begin at dawn. You remember it had been snowing for several days; but it had stopped the night before, and they had begun clearing the roads. The sun's coming up.

EMILY: There's Main Street . . . why, that's Mr. Morgan's drug-store before he changed it! . . . And there's the livery stable. . . . Oh, that's the town I knew as a little girl. And, *look,* there's the old white fence that used to be around our house. Oh, I'd forgotten that! Oh, I loved it so! Are they inside?

STAGE MANAGER: Yes, your mother'll be coming downstairs in a minute to make breakfast.

As it turns out, Emily's visit is not sweet, for she can no longer make a difference, but only watch the world go by.

EMILY: I can't. I can't go on. It goes so fast. We don't have time to look at one another. I didn't realize. So all that was going on and we never noticed. Take me back—up the hill—to my grave. But first: Wait! One more look. Good-by. Good-by, world. Good-by, Gro-ver's Corners . . . Mama and Papa. Good-by to clocks ticking . . . and Mama's sunflowers. And food and coffee. And new-ironed dresses and hot baths . . . and sleeping and waking up. . . . Do any human beings ever realize life while they live it?—every, every minute?

One of her dead companions replies, "Now you know! That's what it was to be alive. To move about in a cloud of ignorance; to go up and down trampling on the feelings of those . . . of those about you. To spend and waste time as though you had a million years."

Such a life—unexamined, unappreciated, and soon over—may indeed, in retrospect, seem empty, even meaningless. But not if we take the same set of pictures, select them, arrange them, mount and treasure them while we can, and then pass them on—today, not after our loved ones (or we) are gone. When we do these things thoughtfully and considerately, patterns of meaning begin to emerge.

We are free to choose, and therefore free to change and grow, with each passing day. We are also free to use our memories in ways that will invest our lives with meaning, sustaining rather than diminishing our self-image and, accordingly, our hopes. We can dwell on our failures or losses, refusing to let go of the darker sides of our past; this is like saving only the pictures we hate, darkening our walls, ruining our scrapbooks. Or we can do the opposite and keep alive fond memories. Each of us has loved a spouse, parent, or friend who is lost to us in death. We can remember the love or dwell on the loss. As John C. Meagher writes, "Tell me what you keep as your historical landmarks, what pictures are in your private album, and I will tell you who you are. But I remind you that you are, in substantial part, who you choose to be."

As we arrange the pictures of our life, we choose the images we wish to remember. While pressing them in our scrapbook, we might also take the time to crack open and dust off a half-forgotten page, to lovingly reflect on earlier seasons gone by: departed loved ones' smiles and sparkling eyes; friends who left this world before us; grandparents, parents, spouses, sometimes, sadly, even children. Whether saved in a book or fixed in memory, these are the pictures of our lives, our most precious keepsakes—most precious, because they remind us that we are what we love.

2. Self-Portraits

It is something to be able to paint a particular picture,
or to carve a statue, and so to make a few objects
beautiful; but it is far more glorious to carve and paint
the very atmosphere and medium through which we
look, which morally we can do. To affect the quality of
the day, that is the highest of arts.

—*Henry David Thoreau,* WALDEN

Imagine this. You are living in a world constituted almost entirely
of warmth, water, and darkness. Food and shelter are free. Life
demands nothing of you. Yet daily you grow, develop, and change.
As you grow, your world slowly becomes smaller, more constric-
tive. Finally, you are too big for your world; it will no longer con-
tain you. When this time comes, not so much by an act of will as
by necessity, you break free. Entering a dark tunnel and moving
toward the light, in a matter of moments you enter a new world.
Your life changes forever. The world you enter also changes by
your entrance. Within minutes, into your world brightness, dry-
ness, and hunger are introduced. As for the world you enter, in
quick measure you both subtract from and add to its quotient of
suffering and of joy.

Whether born in a manger and destined for greatness, or born,

as I was, at St. Luke's Hospital in Boise, Idaho, this part of the
story barely differs from one successful birth to another: out of the
darkness, into the light; out of the womb, into the world and into
the wildness.

In almost every sense, human birth is wild: we enter the world
untamed; the world we enter is filled with unpredictability; and,
the odds against our being born in the first place are so crazy that,
save in retrospect, no thinking person an eon, millennium, or even
a century ago would risk the untold billions to one odds against the
very human being who turned out to be us actually being born.

Think about it this way:

1. We are born wild. To one degree or another, our hungers and
passions will be tamed, but we come into the world not as prospec-
tive model citizens but as primal, sense-driven creatures. Those
who believe that children are born pure and innocent, only to be
corrupted by society, either haven't had children of their own or
paid no attention to them during their first two years. An infant is
all id, a two-year-old all id and ego. This makes good, practical
sense. The world is much less predictable than the womb. For an
infant, naked selfishness and raw importunateness are tantamount
to survival, leading us to recognize that

2. The life into which we are born is filled with an unimaginable
range of possibility. Even to the most prescient embryo, life on
earth begins as something completely unexpected. From that day
forth, it continues to be confoundingly unpredictable.

When one of my parishioners, seeking to make rational sense of
an irrational tragedy, tries to fix blame on him- or herself or on others by asking "What did I do to deserve this?" I almost always
respond by answering "Nothing." They did nothing to deserve having a plane fall out of the sky on its way to Paris with their daughter
in seat 14B. They also did nothing to deserve being put in the posi-

tion to suffer the pain they feel, since none of us did anything to deserve being born in the first place, a reminder that

3. It's crazy that we are even here to ask these questions. Every birth is a wild card, the result of untold billions of consecutive throws of the genetic dice. Not only did all of our ancestors somehow manage to live to puberty and couple, but also in each instance the single one of millions of sperm that carried what ultimately would become the coding for our genes had to make it first to the right egg.

We take this for granted, but I will wager that you would say I was absolutely mad if I told you I was going to choose one of several hundred million balls in a lottery to be repeated several million times and that every single time my number would come up. In both your life and mine, this is precisely what happened. How little we have done to deserve being born in the first place, and how utterly astonishing it is that we find ourselves in this amazing life able to wonder what it means.

If we are lucky enough to enjoy and struggle through life's stages—infancy, youth, adolescence, young adulthood, maturity, old age—we get many opportunities to discover who we are. Not that this is even possible. Of the three conundrums Gauguin posed in his Tahitian triptych (*Where did we come from? Who are we? Where are we going?*), though the second may seem the most tractable, questions of individual identity have bedeviled philosophers for centuries.

Is our individual identity, or selfhood, over time constituted by memory retention, the reservoir of our remembered experiences? Does it lie in the spatiotemporal continuity of our body from birth to death? Or, as Kant suggests, is it some sort of transcendental unity inseparable from perception? The further philosophers delve, the more abstruse their reflections become. No answer really

[27]

works. Memory is the best. Yet, in linking our experiences of self over time, memory often fails us, or deludes us in creative reconstruction. The continuity of our physical identity is no more certain a measure, given that our bodies re-create themselves almost daily. John Locke writes in his *Essay Concerning Human Understanding* that if our soul and body are one, " 'twill be impossible, in that constant flux of the Particles of our Bodies, that any Man should be the same Person, two days, or two moments together." As for some metaphysical idea of self that might offer the key to our innermost being, we are left with a word (*soul*) that completely eludes definition.

The search for individual identity is clearly more promising in concept than in actuality. However central they may seem to a successful quest for meaning, answers in response to the question "Who am I?" load the coffers of our understanding with fool's gold. This is because "Who am I?" is an adolescent question.

Adolescence consists in breaking free. Beginning our lives wholly dependent, and then for a time constrained by parental strictures, once out of the blocks, in trying to discover our "authentic self," we naturally jump from goal to goal, responding to this stimulus or that, embracing one idea and then another. Adolescents are "indiscriminate evaluators." Over time, we winnow our experiments into more sustained endeavors—often from many sexual relationships to one dedicated relationship, from many vocational possibilities to a single job, from quicksilver intellectual passions to a more sustained set of values about the world and our place in it. At the end of this process, and for very good reason, ideally we will ask "How am I doing?" and "How can I do it better?" rather than waste time pondering who we are.

Adolescence plays a critical role in human development. In our adolescent years we initiate, if awkwardly and often hurtfully, what may turn out to be lifelong trajectories or arcs of meaning. We make mistakes our parents would not make for us, but the passage from dependence to autonomy requires that we begin to take our own risks and fail in our own ways.

During my own adolescence, my father once told me that a bumblebee is biggest when first hatched. This may be true of bumblebees, but I certainly didn't feel that big. My father forgot that he was still far bigger, as all parents are. Undeniably, to discover sex and practice freedom, to break out of orbit and explore the world on one's own, is a heady thing. As long as it is age appropriate, there is nothing wrong with adolescence. Leash the passion of adolescence to the experience of adulthood, and we might infuse practicality with excitement while tempering excess by prudence. Exuberant, well-grounded people manage to do this. Most of us err either by curbing adventure or, conversely, by failing to grow up.

Yet, as a window on life's meaning, adolescence remains the perfect starting place. Never are we more preoccupied with who we are and what life means. Ups are higher, downs are lower. Once completely freed from the umbilical cord, we focus on our belly buttons.

It is useful to remember that, in harder times, adolescence barely existed. People often began working during childhood, tended to marry early (assuming the mantle of adulthood without enjoying the pleasures and experiencing the pain of untrammeled youth), and then died in what passes today as early middle age. Those who profess nostalgia for a simpler age might contemplate this. Things may have gone to hell lately—each succeeding generation has thought so since the beginning of time—but today's hell is far preferable to yesterday's imagined heaven. We forget how short the lifespan was before this century. Some two millennia ago, meeting death at the age of thirty-three, both Alexander the Great and Jesus beat the odds. In the United States, at the turn of the last century, life expectancy was forty-seven.

Born into a less demanding world, my friends and I extended our adolescence late into our twenties, sometimes well beyond. The baby-boomer generation knows more about adolescence than any generation in history, because we had the opportunity to prolong our adolescence further into adulthood than any previous generation. Bumblebees stay big longer today than they once did. Questions like "Who am I?" can preoccupy us for years.

If, from late childhood on, I had to get up at five in the morning and work without ceasing until dark simply to survive, I'd consider supper and a beer to be a bargain. My projects, and thus my identity, would be a given. Questions like "Who am I?" and "What does life mean?" are therefore a luxury. People may have asked them since the beginning of time, but today we have more time to ponder them. If seducing from our lives an extended measure of adolescent angst, the luxury to ponder ultimate questions is not a bad thing. On the other hand, since, by its very nature, adolescence is marked by self-absorption, our answers to these questions may be further from the mark than were those of our less-privileged ancestors.

Let me share a story from my own adolescence. To aid my search for life's meaning, thirty years ago, while interning at Stanford University's Memorial Church, I followed a strict ascetic regimen. I went to bed at one, awoke at five, and spent each morning drinking Lapsang souchong tea and reading Greek philosophy. Every afternoon I served as guru and guide to a few ragtag disciples. Evenings I listened to Mahler and read Milton, which, together with the Vietnam War, were the primary sources for my budding eschatological vision.

Should you doubt that I was taking my life too seriously, for a

week or two in the late spring of that year, I took off my glasses
when walking around campus, so as not to lust after gorgeous half-
dressed women. Since I am almost blind, this plan proved imprac-
tical. I lapsed and returned to lust. But I maintained my other dis-
ciplines. My goal was to learn Latin and Greek and to read all of
Western philosophy in two years. What better way to discover
the truth! I cut off all my hair, grew a foot-long beard, lost thirty
pounds, made it to the Stoics, and collapsed. Positive that I'd con-
tracted consumption or some equally romantic nineteenth-century
disease, I went to the university health service. My doctor was not
impressed. She said that I had been behaving like an idiot. There
was absolutely nothing wrong with me that a little more sleep and a
little less tea wouldn't cure. She told me that she never wanted to
see me again. I never wanted to see her again either, so I abandoned
my quest for perfection.

Recently, Wayne Rood, Acting Dean of the Chapel at Stanford
when I worked there, told me, "When you were on your ascent of
the mystical mountain, I considered firing you because you weren't
doing your job, forcing the rest of us to cover your work in addition
to doing ours." Even had I recognized the impact of my search for
meaning on other people's lives, my then overweening sense of self-
importance might have led me to take offense at Wayne's concerns.
I understand them now. When we follow our own bliss at the
expense of interpersonal responsibilities, we must measure personal gains in one project against shared losses in others. This is
not a zero-sum game. When duty is sacrificed on the altar of self-
absorption, even the worshiper loses.

At least my adolescent behavior had the charm of being age-
appropriate. Such antics are less appealing when the search for
"self" in adulthood leads the seeker straight into the thicket of self-
absorption. Even as adolescents need to become "themselves" to

gain autonomy, adults discover meaning by connecting. As long as we confuse the search for meaning with the search for selfhood, we are wanderers in the woods. Inexorably, such a search leads to narcissism.

You surely know the story of Narcissus, a beautiful boy who refused to love others and was therefore condemned to love no one but himself. In one version of this ancient myth, Narcissis wasted away longing after his reflection, mirrored in a still, deep pool; in another, he leaned over to embrace it, fell in, and drowned. In both tellings this picturesque Greek legend warns against the dangers of self-love.

As a teenager, I threw the term *narcissist* around long before I knew its source. Narcissists were people who skipped lunch in order to have a full half-hour to comb their hair. They came to school not so much to learn as to be seen. Narcissists were the kids you tried to remember not to ask, "How are you?" It was their favorite subject. We called them stuck up and made fun of them behind their backs. But many of us also secretly envied them, because they seemed so pleased with themselves. Back then I didn't realize how insecure they were, that this was simply their way of compensating. My way of compensating was to disappear into my locker whenever a pretty girl walked by.

The word *narcissism* took on greater significance in the 1970s. Sociologist Christopher Lasch wrote a book on the narcissistic trends in our culture, coining the term "the me generation." Robert Ringer's *Looking Out for Number One* soared to the top of the best-seller charts. Self-love and the quest for pleasure, summed up in the dismissive but apt "He who dies with the most toys wins," became troubling emblems of an entire generation. Call it the "Adolescent Generation."

Drawing on personal experience and insights from my counseling, I know now that narcissism is more than self-love. Since, by definition, narcissism reflects unhealthy self-absorption, the narcissistic danger most of us face springs not from self-love but from self-doubt, even from self-hatred. Suicide is a narcissistic act. People become so completely absorbed in their troubles that the only way they can imagine solving them is to paint themselves out of their own self-portrait. We are far more likely to be absorbed by negative self-images than positive ones.

"What will he think of me?"
"How do I look?"
"If I speak, will I say something stupid?"

And then, an hour later:

"He must have thought I was an idiot."
"God, I looked terrible."
"How could I have said such a stupid thing."

This is narcissism in its most familiar form.

A bit of personal testimony, embarrassing but true. When I walk into a room full of strangers, my hands seem to grow. There I am, trying to act naturally, pretending that I know what I'm doing, only to be thwarted by these increasingly conspicuous hands. What should I do with them? For those of you—I hope there are not many—who have this particular problem, the best thing to do is to tuck your hands into your pockets or put them behind your back and pretend to read something on a bulletin board. As you do, remember this: you are not the only self-absorbed person in the room. When we look into the deep, still pool, one sure way to avoid recoiling at our own reflection is to contemplate our shared humanity, to see ourselves in others and others in us. I am not offering a cure for human awkwardness here, only suggesting ways to avoid the pitfalls of self-abasement.

As long as we perceive ourselves as a fixed self or identity rather than as a consortium of personae that take turns appearing on our stage, we will think either too highly or too lowly of ourselves. Both misperceptions throw us out of balance. If each of our personalities is made up of an amalgam of traits, they are also composed—not perfectly but tellingly—by memory. We remember—literally "put back together"—who we are. So, if one of your selves misbehaves, don't overreact. Just call for reinforcements.

I admit, to muster allies for life's battles is easier said than done. Given our multiplicity of selves, confusion abounds. This is true for all of us. The essayist Lewis Thomas, a sometime parishioner of mine before his death a few years ago, confessed to having more selves than he could possibly count or keep track of. In his essay "Selves" in *The Medusa and the Snail*, Thomas admitted that "to be truthful there have been a few times when they were all there at once, like those girls on television, clamoring for attention, whole committees of them, a House Committee, a Budget Committee, a Grievance Committee, even a Committee on Membership, although I don't know how any of them ever got in. No chairman, ever, certainly not me. At the most I'm a sort of administrative assistant. There's never an agenda. At the end I bring the refreshments."

Since we change according to mood, task, role, and company, each of us has multiple personae. Sometimes they collaborate (as in Lewis Thomas's committee), and sometimes, often less than helpfully, one takes the field all by itself. As I mentioned above, every time I talk to my mother on the phone, the little boy in me threatens to misbehave or seek approval. This same little boy inconveniently reappears when I confuse my wife with my mother, something, from hard-won experience, I don't recommend.

Not that you can always help it. You may have seen this article in the paper: "A Wisconsin psychiatrist convinced a patient she had 120 separate personalities—including those of a duck and the devil—and then charged her for group therapy." Happily, most of us are less interesting than this patient, and most therapists less creative in their billing. But when it comes to past lives, even multiple lives, we don't have to trace our lineage back to Cleopatra's court to encounter a full array of predecessors.

Half hidden here is a theological point. None of us is an individual pure and simple. We each are a nexus of relationships and roles. By the same token, our bodies are a colony of cells and organs, with every part, unbeknownst to the others, stamped with the same DNA. Perhaps the living system on this planet, both the human ecosystem and the whole shebang, is also a collaborative, if not always mutually cooperative, whole, each part intimately related to the others, shaped and changed in relationship. "One body, many members," as St. Paul put it. Together we constitute an interdependent web of being. In the most capacious sense, from sagebrush to sage, these multifaceted colonies and systems are related in a way that neither they nor we are conscious of, each living part and living system marked, perhaps, by the DNA of God.

In more practical terms, no $10 million house has as much intrinsic value as a barn raising, where all the people in a community gather for a day and build a barn on one of their properties. At the end of the day, folks don't go home and feel diminished because one of their neighbors' barns is now bigger or newer than their own. They go home and feel good about the ways their community has been enhanced, and about the part they played. When neighbors get together to raise a barn (or more often these days through Habitat for Humanity or the Enterprise Foundation to raise a house), they don't eliminate poverty. All they do is help a neighbor. But the meal at the end of the day is far more festive and satisfying than that of a billionaire who will never have enough. As John Ruskin wrote, "The ultimate reward for human toil is not what we get for it, but what we become by it."

Because the key to identity is not selfhood but integration, the question "How am I doing (or connecting)?" speaks volumes more than "Who am I?" even with respect to who we are. When we integrate our values, projects, and relationships, our lives cohere.

The great French postimpressionist Cézanne said that "we live in a rainbow of chaos." So long as the rainbow is in place—a trajectory from who we are to whom we are striving to become—the order in its arc and pattern of its colors will temper the chaos around us.

Meaning begins to emerge.

3. Character and Plot

*We can act as if there were a God; feel as if we were
free; consider Nature as if she were full of special
designs; lay plans as if we were to be immortal; and
we find then that these words do make a genuine
difference in our moral life.   —William James,*
THE VARIETIES OF RELIGIOUS EXPERIENCE

*What is art if not a concentrated and impassioned
effort to make something with the little we have, the
little we see?   —Andre Dubus,*
MEDITATIONS FROM A MOVABLE CHAIR

In his prologue to the novel *Damien,* Hermann Hesse says that our
individual lives constitute a story. Each of our stories, both unique
and remarkable, happen once, never again. Of his own life, Hesse
writes, "My story is not a pleasant one; it is neither sweet nor har-
monious, as invented stories are; [my story] has the taste of non-
sense and chaos, of madness and dreams—like the lives of all who
stop deceiving themselves."

In the 1960s, Hesse was acclaimed by a generation who greeted
his writings with quasi-worshipful enthusiasm. He was appealing
because he was an "adolescent" author, one who dedicated his novels to the angst and drama of self-discovery. By strength of numbers, adolescents ruled the roost in the sixties. Searching for
meaning as an adolescent might, Hesse wrung it (even negative
meanings such as "life is absurd") from the clouds of self-

[37]

absorption. With Nietzschean flourish, he pitched to his audience, I among them, wonderful images of climbing to the mountaintop and standing alone, naked in the storm, defiant against the fates.

Shortly after Hesse became my all-time favorite author, I concluded that I would die before the age of twenty-five. My father had cancer when he was twenty-five. Given three months to live, he staged a remarkable recovery and then went on to serve for twenty-four years in the U.S. Senate. By cultivating this death fantasy, I may have been substituting myself as a sacrifice due to the gods in exchange for his life. More likely, I subconsciously determined that the best way to avoid competing with my very successful father was to check out before I had a chance to fail.

Knowing that I would die before the age of twenty-five had distinct advantages. Untrammeled by the responsibilities of growing up, I could skip class whenever I wished and devote my brief life to the pleasures of marijuana and the writing of incomprehensible poetry. I had only one goal: to seize and exaggerate every opportunity for pain and joy. By the way, they were wonderful years. I wouldn't turn them back for anything.

Not all projects are discrete, with a beginning, middle, and end. Many are like leitmotivs, especially those that wend their way thematically from year to year, investing our lives with shape and meaning. In the theater a "through line" is a theme that runs throughout an entire play, connecting its sometimes disparate parts. In my own life, the through line is "love and death." I almost lost my father when I was a baby, when I was in my first year of college my grandfather died, and my best friend died during our sophomore year. So I can see where my through line comes from. And yet, back then, I wasn't so much facing my own death as entertaining a fantasy of death. Both love and death remained in chrysalis.

Nevertheless, this caricature of mortal combat—a single human being, self-conscious, undeluded, alone in the cosmos, shaking both fists at the stars—sealed my decision to pursue the study of religion. Not that I was interested in the ministry. Nothing could have been further from my mind. My goal was to hone the truth, however hard its edge. At Harvard, my academic specialty was heretics. I had a great affinity for heretics. Even though I had to learn Coptic, I wrote my doctoral dissertation on a heretical gospel, the Gospel of Thomas. I especially loved the fact that it didn't make it into the Bible.

Having passed the age of twenty-five without mortal incident, I finally had to settle on a career. I would teach religion. Not only that, but I would be a superior, far more objective teacher of religion than most of my colleagues, because my critical capacities were completely unclouded by a belief in God.

As they unfold over time, one saving aspect of our life stories is that we don't write them alone. Almost everyone we encounter coscripts them, our plots often turning on events outside of our control. Chance encounters open new doors or close old ones, yet the through line remains. This doesn't necessarily lend our lives a sense of coherence. Our through line may be chaos. Even when it's not, at times we lose our way. The plot of our lives has a will of its own. In my case, several mentors and the God I didn't believe in played a trick on me. I ended up in the parish ministry.

At the beginning of my ministry, I believed in belief and even in believers, but I didn't quite yet believe in God. After more than twenty years of shared ministry with my congregation—after hundreds of deaths and even more rebirth—not only do I believe in God, but today, in one sense, I believe only in God. Everything else is too small. Only an ultimate reality far beyond the compass of our own existence can invest our limited, fragile, often broken lives with full significance.

[39]

God doesn't exist because we need God. We exist because the universe is so amazing that only something like the idea of God can begin to come close to comprehending it. As Dag Hammarskjöld wrote, "God does not die on the day when we cease to believe in a personal deity, but we die on the day when our lives cease to be illumined by the steady radiance, renewed daily, of a wonder, the source of which is beyond all reason."

For me, the God project is more meaning-laden than any other dimension of lifecraft. "God is really only another artist," Pablo Picasso said. But God's creation is by far the greatest masterpiece of all. To interpret it, we have to begin with ourselves. The reason is simple. We are not only interpreters of God's masterpiece but also part of the story we interpret.

One way to discover meaning is to view our own chapter of the story—given its length and breadth—as we might a novel, sorting out character and plot, trying to make sense of both. A difficult plot does not preclude the development of strong character; often the opposite is true. Also, by demonstrating character, we can sort our plots out, choosing among the projects that invest our lives with meaning, even when life turns against us. Finally, to a degree at least, character shapes plot. The little engine that could often does; engines that can't rarely do.

When we break the plot of our lives into discrete episodes or themes that run throughout our story, meanings that might otherwise be obscured may reveal themselves. To illustrate this, let me share several stories from life, some familiar, others not.

In the weeks following Princess Diana's death, many people in counseling, especially women, devoted their therapeutic hour to unpacking their feelings about her. What did this have to do with them? Evidently a great deal. These women were exploring Princess Diana's story in order to discover and create meaning in their own lives. They wanted to avoid her mistakes (vicariously their own), spare her from her enemies (vicariously their own), and understand the meaning of her death (vicariously their own). Such projects are central to lifecraft. We observe the lives of others, identify with them, and sometimes try to copy them. We attempt to learn from their mistakes, or resist our temptation to make the same ones.

I don't believe in fairy princesses. When Princess Diana died, I refused to concede more to the death of someone I had always dismissed as a fashion plate than to that of a forgotten young woman in East Harlem, who surely died the very same week and left two children whose names we shall probably never know. On the day of Diana's funeral, my wife set her alarm for 6:00 in the morning in order to watch it live. I tried to sleep in, continuing, even wanting to believe, that what was happening had nothing to do with me. I was wrong. Precisely because her story had such universal impact, pondering Diana's life and death gave billions of people the opportunity to reflect on the meaning of their own.

When I finally joined my wife in front of the television, the first thing that struck me was her tears. Don't argue with tears. They come from someplace deep. They almost always matter. I finally got it. The little envelope on Diana's casket that said "Mummy"; the song by Elton John; Prime Minister Tony Blair reading 1 Corinthians 13 as it has almost never been read before; and then Diana's brother, Lord Spencer, who spoke the truth, his love expressed in anger. I was now crying too. Despite her "meaningless" death, I began to reflect on what meanings Diana might have discovered and created in her life.

Previously, I had seen no relationship between her life and mine. I read her obituary in the papers and a few of the pundits' postmortems, mostly depicting a vain life and senseless demise. The question remained. Why did this woman touch so many hearts so deeply? Only when her brother spoke did I begin to understand. No one had put it as clearly. She touched so many hearts because she felt unworthy.

By empathy—entering another person's story, its character and plot—we discover meaning in our own story. Empathy suggests that we are not toy soldiers, standing alone on little lead bases, moving ourselves or being moved across a tabletop until someone knocks us over and takes us off the board. That's not the way our stories work. Anything that brings us together—inspiring us to open our hearts, hands, or minds, to forget our differences for a moment and remember we are one—is a sacrament.

To wrench meaning from your own sense of unworthiness, consider Diana's story. She touched the untouchables, first children with AIDS, then lepers, finally land-mine victims without limbs. Suffering from bulimia and a desperate willingness to give love to anyone who would offer kindness in return, she paid a heavy price along the way. Yet this unbelievably beautiful woman, who had so little confidence in herself, somehow managed to give confidence to others. By shifting our angle of vision, meanings emerge from our lives that their plots don't suggest.

You may have seen that picture of Princess Diana with Mother Teresa in the South Bronx taken less than two months before they both died, such very different people save in this respect: each found her place in a caste system—Windsor and Brahmin—and refused to be governed by it. Instead, by embracing the constituency of the rejected, they let their humanity shine through. Diana was born into the English aristocracy, and in many ways she suffered from her privileged birth. Mother Teresa chose the system she entered and didn't seem to have a sense of unworthiness. Some even claim the opposite. But to her public, she too embodied humility.

Humility is not always born from saintliness. It can spring from a sense of unworthiness, which is even more remarkable. A woman has everything anyone could want other than love and self-esteem, perhaps the only things we should hope for in this life. And so what does she do? She gives her love to others and builds their self-esteem. In a zero-sum game, the result would be nothing. In life, it can mean everything. Empty yourself and be filled. Lose yourself and be found. Give and you shall receive, but it's more important that you give. With every gift of self the world is changed.

Never trust how a story appears. Character and plot often diverge. When this beautiful person died, the beauty lost had nothing to do with her looks. As often is the case with physically beautiful people, her looks were as much a personal curse as a boon. This was a woman who apparently hated what she saw when she looked into the mirror. But when she looked into the mirror of other people's eyes, she recognized their pain.

A sense of unworthiness is not the same thing as humility. When people who feel unworthy are humiliated, self-absorption displaces compassion. The distinction is important, because many of us feel unworthy when we measure ourselves against others, our parents' expectations, or people more successful than we are in work or love. Yet, even as humiliated people are abased, humble people often manage to abound. Princess Di's death was tragic not because her promise was unfulfilled but because in part it was fulfilled and might have continued to be fulfilled. Not her promise of happiness, the fairy tale princess story we were invited to believe in, but the larger promise of love given, if never fully received.

Because of her position, beauty, and grace (even because of her public vulnerability), this woman was larger than life. Tiny Mother Teresa also was larger than life. History allots only one or two saints every generation, public saints at least. Yet there are saints everywhere doing Mother Teresa's business. She was different only because of her fame, but rare therefore, because fame does everything it can to destroy sainthood. Though both women were larger than life, Diana is the one I finally can relate to. I relate to her because of her sense of unworthiness. This and her triumph, not over but in spite of it.

What does this have to do with us? Surprisingly, a great deal. We admire other people's strength, but when it comes right down to it, their weakness strikes a closer chord. We don't identify with Princess Diana because she was royal, or because she was beautiful. We identify with her because we could see our tears in her eyes.

In Diana's case, the plot of her life, superficially enviable but in fact destructive of what little confidence she may have had, appears to have spurred a development of character. Inversely, demonstrating character when we suffer misfortune can help us sort our plot lines out. Choosing from among those plots—or projects—that invest our lives with meaning, we can sustain a meaningful existence even when life turns dark.

Sportswriter Christine Brennan tells the story of professional quarterback Mark Rypien of the Washington Redskins. Rypien was voted the Super Bowl Most Valuable Player in 1991. Long after his glory days, he was playing for the Los Angeles Rams in 1997 when his three-year-old son was diagnosed with a brain tumor. During the day, Rypien practiced with his team; at night he slept on a cot at his son's bedside in the hospital. The following year, his son's tumor returned with a vengeance. When he and his wife learned that their child was dying, she was diagnosed with ovarian cancer.

"Why is this happening?" Mark Rypien asked in his conversation with the reporter. "But at the same time," he said, "you've got two people in need, so you make the decision you need to make and move on."

To be with his wife and take care of his son during the last months of the boy's life, Rypien quit football and returned to his Idaho home. His son's favorite restaurant, Chuck E. Cheese, was twenty miles away, but he took his family there every day for lunch. On August 22, 1998, having fallen asleep on his parents' bed, lying between them, Rypien's son died.

When Christine Brennan called to see how the family was coping, Mark Rypien told her that his wife's cancer was in remission. There was laughter in the background. They were having a party. He was thinking of going back into football.

As life challenges us to do, when tragedy struck, Rypien dropped some projects and concentrated on others. Not that he could change this sad chapter of his life. To save his son was beyond his mortal power. But by focusing on his father project and husband project, Mark Rypien tackled those things that had the best chance of redeeming whatever was left of his loved ones' days.

We learn the art of meaning from family stories as well. For me, my father's life is central to my understanding of life's potential and fragility. Frank Church almost died of cancer when he was twenty-five years and I three months old. Henceforth, he threw all caution to the wind, taking every chance he could with life, especially with his career. When my father turned thirty, he and my mother sold our house; we moved in with my mother's parents, and, against almost everyone's advice, he embarked on a quixotic quest for a seat in the U.S. Senate. Amazingly the little engine that believed it could, did. At thirty-two, Frank Church became the youngest senator.

His doctors told him that the experimental and very heavy course

of radiation that killed his cancer would likely take years off the
end of his life. They were right. Frank Church died at fifty-nine. At
his funeral I said, "Because my father was not afraid to die, he was
not afraid to live. He did not spend his life, as so many of us do, little by little until he was gone. He gave it away to others. He invested
it in things that would ennoble and outlast him."

My father taught me that we can change life's plot by demonstrating character. Both of us learned this same lesson from his father-
in-law, my maternal grandfather, the richest man in the world. I
know this because whenever I visited his home, he would slip me a
five-dollar bill. "Spend it on anything you want," he'd say, "but
don't tell your parents."

Chase Clark was a short man with twinkling eyes and a shock of
white hair. When he was two, his family moved to Idaho from Indi-
ana. Some sixty years later, the people of Idaho elected him governor. That isn't what made him special. His character made him
special: a self-educated lawyer who specialized in everything from
shotgun weddings to moonshine, he often bought his clients new
boots so that they wouldn't catch cold in jail.

My grandparents had already lost one child at the end of a difficult pregnancy. When my grandmother got pregnant again, Chase,
concerned about her health, closed his law practice. They moved
to Salt Lake City, where the hospitals were much better, and for the
next six months, waited together for my mother to be born. Had
Chase not done this, almost surely my grandmother would have
died, and my mother would not have been born. By setting his priorities and demonstrating character, my grandfather changed the
plot of all of our lives.

Chase's law practice didn't suffer. Neither did his pocketbook.
Having accepted land in lieu of fees, he owned tens of thousands of
acres, many of them in the Stanley Basin near Sun Valley. But his

money didn't last. At the time of the first great Wall Street crash, Chase Clark was a member of the board of the largest bank in Macky, Idaho. His bank folded as a casualty of the Depression. Keeping only his ranch, he sold all his land at dirt prices, personally making good on every small investor's holding. Not all good deeds are punished. My grandfather became a hero. Again character drove plot. Shortly thereafter, he became mayor of Idaho Falls, and in 1940, Chase Clark was elected governor of Idaho.

In 1942, a Catholic priest, pleading for action to redress the growing problem of overcrowding in the state penitentiary, approached Governor Clark. There were nearly three times as many prisoners as the penitentiary was built to hold. Murderers were sharing cells with pickpockets. Three months before he would stand for reelection, my grandfather pardoned more than one hundred prisoners. As far as we can tell, only two of those he pardoned ever returned to prison—and at least one showed up for his funeral in 1966—but the issue his opponent had been praying for had presented itself. Persuaded that it was no longer safe to walk the streets at night, the voters turned against him, and he lost the election by four hundred votes.

Chase Clark might have become president. My grandfather was one of the western politicians whom Franklin Delano Roosevelt was considering as a possible vice presidential candidate to replace Henry Wallace in 1944. As the only major Democrat to lose in what was otherwise a Democratic landslide, Governor Clark was eliminated from contention. Two years later, Roosevelt chose Harry Truman.

As FDR's very last major presidential appointment, my grandfather lived out his days as Idaho's federal court judge. In 1966, when the richest man in the world died, he left almost nothing in his will. Even my parents couldn't understand. But then they looked through his books. For years, at the end of every month, he had cleaned out his accounts: fifty dollars here, twenty dollars there. Everything he didn't need for food or mortgage payments he gave away to good causes and derelict relatives.

Now I know—and it was to my delight as a child—why my grand-father's desk drawers were chock-full of trinkets. When a Boys' Club in Omaha would send him a plastic teepee or an American flag lapel pin, he would respond with a check. Maybe he was the richest man in the world after all. True wealth is measured not by what we leave behind but by what we can afford to give away before we go.

Chase Clark was not a scholar, but one philosopher who might have appealed to him was William James. In down-home language, James, an American pragmatist, wrote about the ways in which we discover and create meaning. He called himself a radical empiri-cist: radical because he refused to accept that there certainly was a God, an empiricist because he learned from everything he experi-enced. James had little patience for those of his contemporaries who claimed that with one hundred moves they could solve life's Rubik's Cube. "Objective evidence and certitude are doubtless very fine ideals to play with," he wrote, "but where on this moonlit and dream-visited planet are they found?"

James held that our beliefs can be self-ratifying. For instance, if we fall in love and believe that we would be the best possible partner for the person we have fallen in love with, our faith can sometimes move mountains. I can attest to this. "Who gains promo-tions, boons, appointments, but the man in whose life they are seen to play the part of live hypotheses?" James asks. "His faith acts on the powers above him as a claim, and creates its own verification." Or it doesn't. There is also a will to disbelieve. The little engine either can or it can't. "If your heart does not want a world of moral

[48]

reality," James writes, "your head will assuredly never make you believe in one."

In her book *Working on God,* Winifred Gallagher quotes the Zen master Shunryu Suzuki's definition of human freedom: "If it is possible to go one mile to the east, that means it is possible to go one mile to the west." This also suggests that it may not be possible to go two miles in either direction. In pursuing major projects this is critical information. Recognizing limits is as important as believing in our ability to reach our limits. The trick lies in choosing the right projects and trusting in our ability to succeed. Too often we do the opposite. Rather than believing in what we can do, we end up dissatisfied with what we do not have or who we cannot be. Our cup is half empty. Disappointment almost always follows wishful thinking. Try reversing the words. Call it "thoughtful wishing." Think to be who you can be, do what you can do, and have what you can have. Your cup is now half full.

Conversely, by failing to believe in our ability to create and discover meaning, we succumb to two seductive sins. I call these the sin of sophisticated resignation and the sin of cynical chic. First, we recognize how intractable life's problems are and resign ourselves to them; this is sophisticated resignation. Then, not wanting to be perceived as naive, we dismiss dreamers and idealists as innocents; this is cynical chic. Both make perfect sense. They also serve as tombstones for wishful thinkers whom disappointment has led to hopelessness. In the old children's game of "paper, scissors, stone," sophisticated resignation is paper over scissors, cynical chic, scissors over stone.

It is in our nature to be dissatisfied with what we have: our work, looks, and health, our sex lives, the state of the world, the length of our vacations, the size of our houses, the way we live. We run up against limits everywhere. We can't always do what we dream of

[49]

doing. Nor can we always have what we fantasize about having or be who we wish to be. Each limit reminds us of our mortality, the bar that is placed on life itself.

Not that limits are bad. They establish value. The scarcer something is, the more precious it becomes. If gold grew on trees and apples were buried deep within the ground, we would count our fortune in apples, not in gold. When King Midas turned his whole world into gold, he became poor. When he could have as much gold as he wanted whenever he wanted it, what he once placed ultimate value on turned out to be worthless.

Maurice Sendak hints at this in his children's story about a pampered dog. This little dog had everything. She had her own pillows, comb, and brush. She had a red wool sweater and two wide windows through which to gaze out on the world. She even had two bowls to eat from and a master who loved her. Despite all this, she left home, explaining, "I am discontented. I want something I do not have. There must be more to life than having everything." The moral is simple. We discover meaning in what we have, what we can do, and in whom we are able to become. Successful projects are those over which we have at least some control. It is by filling in the lines of our own possibility, no matter how tightly drawn, that we discover and create new meaning.

Let me illustrate this with one final tale, the story of Corinna Marsh. Corinna lived in a tiny, grim, happily cluttered apartment in the Marquis Hotel in Manhattan. Back in the late eighties, when I visited her, I had to run a gauntlet of crack pushers. She had resided at the hotel for decades and loved it. She wouldn't move for anything. Not that she could. Corinna had almost no money.

In her last decade, Corinna was legally blind. She had trouble getting around and heard with difficulty. But she knew where everything was, the hanging plants, the teapot, and, most important, her yellow pad on which she scribbled a remarkable body of acid, yet hilarious, verse.

> *When all the malfunctions of old age assail me,*
> *And skills that I've always depended on fail me,*
> *The best way I've found to avoid thoughts of hearses,*
> *Is putting my mind on composing light verses.*

We're not talking Hallmark card material here. No sentimental sunsets or rocking chairs on porches evoking the simple pleasures of old age, with Golden Pond in the background. Just humor and honesty, enough of each to make one wince.

How did she do it? How did she get up every morning and affirm life? In one couplet, she gives her own answer. "I am unusually blest: There's so much to laugh at, I don't get depressed." Corinna didn't develop her wit as a stratagem for coping with the pains of old age. It was her signature for years. Had you asked her about it, she'd have told you, "Don't despair. It's the only thing Bill Buckley and I have in common."

Over the years these remarkable people—Corinna and William F. Buckley—struck up a curious, very appealing relationship. Corinna was a lifelong liberal. To the end of her days, her political opinions remained as strong as they were salty. She had the force of her convictions; she didn't keep them to herself. Disproving the adage that thoughtful people grow more conservative (or more passive) as they get older, over the final twenty years of her life Corinna submitted several conservatively incorrect poems to William F. Buckley's *National Review.* To Buckley's credit, he published almost all of them. One day he invited her to lunch. "Well, Corinna," Buckley said. "I hope you will tell all your liberal friends that I don't bite."

"Sure," she replied. "And I hope you'll tell all your conservative friends that I do."

[51]

She certainly did. When I told her about the movie *Cocoon*, in which a bevy of oldsters recover from the debilities of age and rediscover the pleasures of youth, Corinna's comment was, "Nuts!" I know this cuts against contemporary pieties. In response to the "I'm not getting older, I'm getting better" crowd, Corinna invoked her own statute of limitations. When I made the mistake of telling her that she was getting both older and better, she told me to grow up. Then she sent me this poem.

> *Though living too long can destroy like a pox*
> *And fighting it can be like countering rocks,*
> *There's one thing I must say on God's behalf:*
> *He lets me find whimsy at which I can laugh.*

Corinna died at the age of one hundred. For her tombstone she chose the words "That's that." Never coming close to fooling herself, she created and discovered meaning in her life to the end of her days. Humor was her through line.

4. Tombs and Monuments

If you would see the man's monument, look around.
—*Epitaph of Sir Christopher Wren*

In 1998, my family and I went on a ten-day adventure to Egypt, one of the cradles of civilization. We started out in Giza, took a five-day cruise up the Nile from Luxor to Aswan, spent a morning in Abu Simbel, and then ended our journey in Cairo and what is left of ancient Memphis. Everything we experienced inspired awe. Well, almost everything. One small, if grating, exception was the phonetic translation of my name into hieroglyphics. Church comes out "placenta, chick, mouth, placenta." At least I saved the money I might have spent on a personalized cartouche.

The earliest tomb we visited was near the ancient city of Memphis. More than 4,500 years old and belonging to an important nobleman, its walls were covered with depictions of domestic life, of dancing and dining. One wall depicted jugglers and acrobats, another children at play. Inside was a map of the tomb, giving instructions to the gods on where to find the crypt containing its occupant's mummified remains. Sufficient food was stored to provide sustenance for a long journey, and all his treasures (long since looted by thieves some three to four millennia ago) filled the chambers as in later tombs. But the distinguishing features here, the winning touches, were joyous representations of life on earth, children playing, mother and infant, lavish feasts, and but a very few gods.

Then the strangest thing happened. My family and I were the only people in this tomb. Our guide was masterful at leading us to places just after everyone else had left or right before they arrived. So we were alone in this 4,500-year-old tomb, with all its vivid celebrations of domesticity, when around the corner walks Martha Stewart. Talk about visitations from another world. Entering our tomb was the very woman who boasts intimate knowledge of at least seventy basil vinegars, today's omnipresent advocate of the perfectly decorated life. A little rumpled from the desert, but impeccably dressed in khaki, Martha Stewart joined my completely rumpled family to witness the perfectly decorated death.

However careful his plans—and they were manifestly elaborate—I wonder whether this nobleman was ready for death when the hour came. His preparations were meticulous—the heavenly traffic signs and assembled stores—but was he ready to journey across the sacred waters? Was he better prepared than the slaves who built his tomb, who cut the stones, affixing them so closely that the elements could not invade his sacred sanctuary to disturb his progress or his peace? Was he better prepared than the artisans who carved dancing children, acrobats, jugglers, venison, and amphorae filled with flowing wine on the walls of his sepulchre? For all his power and riches, was this nobleman ready to entrust his heart to the embalmer? Was he more ready than Martha Stewart? More ready than you or I?

What I brought home from Egypt was not a cartouche but an indelible impression of both the weight and fragility of our mortality. Ready or not, whether following a life of fame and fortune or a life of simple labor, each birth comes wrapped in death and each death in mystery.

Religion starts here. It starts at the entrance of the tomb. But then the priests take over. In the tombs of the New Kingdom, in dynasties distinguished by such luminous names as Akhenaton, Nefertiti, Tutankhamen, Ramses II, while unmistakably elaborate, the walls no longer depict domestic scenes and tales from life, but rather they are covered from top to bottom with tales from the afterlife, of meeting Gods, currying their favor, making all the right offerings, establishing their patron's title to immortality. All this is embellished by haunting murals of vanquished enemies from Asia and Africa, depicting beheadings configured to subvert their enemies' vengeful magic and thus prevent them from interrupting the entombed pharaoh's safe passage across the heavenly waters.

Not the pharaoh but the priest is in charge here, the high priest, who knows the right runes, whose power lies in the people's, even in the pharaoh's fear of death. As for the representations of the pharaoh, over time they become more and more gargantuan, monumental, and godlike. How could death possibly prevail? Thirty-five hundred years after his death, Ramses II is still everywhere—Memphis, Luxor, Abu Simbel—three stories high, almighty, demigod-like, awe-inspiring, death-defying, absolute in presumed power, a power both defined and sanctioned by his priests, who conspired with him in his attempt at immortality by marshaling

[55]

one hundred thousand subjects at a time to work and die in the sacred task of erecting his temples—their temples—and his tomb.

On our last day in Egypt, I saw Ramses II face to face. I met him in the mummy room of the great Antiquities Museum in Cairo. He is the second mummy on the right. About 5 foot 4 inches, I would say, well preserved, grave in demeanor, with a wisp of blondish hair. As our son Nathan said, "It looks like the archeologists found him before the Gods did." And yet, in his quest for immortality, what monuments Ramses II, together with his priests, architects, and people, erected.

The second thing I brought home from Egypt is a renewed sense of awe. As ours did, the ancient Egyptians' hearts must have soared at the beauty, audacity, and power expressed by these temples and tombs. We may or may not be immortal, but even if life ends finally with death—the life of the individual extinguished or mysteriously merged with the life of the cosmos—our immortal aspirations remain inspirational. They are ladders to the stars. We can climb them, even ladders built by others, two, three, even four and a half millennia ago. As we identify with their earthbound limitations, we can share their dreams. We can stand in awe of their accomplishments, even as we witness the ash of their earthly remains.

Tombs and monuments can be one and the same. Often our greatest architectural achievements witness to death. Some of the most striking new museums of our own century commemorate victims of the Holocaust. Remembering our dead both honors their memory and triggers our own. We learn from history, pay homage to those who have gone before us, and acknowledge our own mortality. At the same time, we teach ourselves two important lessons: (1) life is complicit with death, and (2) meaning is divined within life's narrow margins.

From our family trip to Egypt, my favorite iconographic image, present from the earliest to the most recent tombs and temples, was the boat. According to ancient Egyptian theology, if we are prepared for the journey, when we die we can take those things we most deeply value across the sea of heaven. Replete with potential provisions, the boat—our lifecraft—is pictured on the walls of our tomb. Keepsakes and treasures are buried nearby that we might have them at the ready when the gods awaken us for our immortal journey.

I love the image of lifecraft as a boat. At times we may feel like a cork with no keel and no momentum. Lacking ballast and sail for the winds to speed us on, we take up space but make no difference, either for ourselves or for others. A ten-year-old in my congregation describes such people as "play date friends, not friends you can go to when you're sad." I would add, not people you would turn to when you want to power a project with collaborative energy. Many people keep their lifecraft safe at harbor. Harbors, too, can be tombs. The high seas may be dangerous, but life itself is dangerous, whether or not we dare live it to the full.

Our sacred vessel extends beyond the tomb in another sense. Whenever we choose to make a reckoning, we can reprovision our lifecraft with things we cherish and set off in a new direction. Not to trivialize the final journey, in every life there are many little births and deaths. If we invest them with power, seize them as opportunities rather than rue them as accidents, our journeys will be more adventuresome and carefully charted than were we simply to be blown by the winds. The trick is to sail out of our tombs while we can.

Such passage is for everyone, not only for noblemen, pharaohs, and priests. We may actually load and redirect our lifecrafts more easily than do rulers and aspiring saints. Not only do we have fewer things to arrange and repack when we set out in a new direction, but also we tend to take ourselves less seriously. This beckons the wind to our sails.

The sage Ramakrishna tells this story. After fourteen years of concentrated effort, the disciple of a great religious master finally gains the power to walk on water. Transported by joy, he turns to his master and says, "Master, come see. At long last I have accomplished my purpose. I can walk on water." To which his master replies, "Fie on it. You have obtained only that which is worth a penny, for that which you have accomplished after fourteen years labor, ordinary mortals do by paying a penny to the boatman."

We can spend a lifetime trying to build a monument, only to find ourselves living in a tomb. To give but one example, we can dedicate ourselves to our work so completely, that other projects get neglected. And then, one day, we may wake up alone, our friends and family having drifted, either literally or figuratively, away from us.

As perilously, we may dedicate our lives only to things we know will please us. This may seem self-serving, but ultimately it is self-limiting. Many people take fewer risks as they grow older, preferring the security of home and television to all the unknown things that might happen if they ventured out into the world. For instance, they could go to see a movie, but it might rain. For many pain avoiders, rain is a dominant life metaphor. On the other hand, if life were a cup half-filled with water, given that our attempts to keep from spilling life's cup lead only to slow evaporation, a little bit of rain might help to fill it up. Jesus invites us to take this one step further, to empty our cup and be filled. Then we can truly say "my cup runneth over."

Let me tell you a story. There was once a woman who had vivid dreams. She would awaken at night and ponder their meanings.

During the daytime she would reflect on her dreams, isolate their symbols, attempt to distill what truth might be in them, and then, through an act of faith—faith in that meaning that ever eludes full explication or final proof—she would try to shape her life by what her dreams had taught her.

Over the years, this woman stopped bothering to arise at night to ponder a vivid dream. There was no apparent need. The meanings were fixed, seeming to require no further elaboration. But then, something cast her life's meaning into question. Perhaps her beloved child or husband died, and her dream interpretations had prepared her not for real but only for imagined death. Or, in her waking hours, maybe she had simply grown older and more practical. Meanings she once had extracted from her dream visions now seemed juvenile. So instead of going back to her dreams, reinterpreting them according to her new experience of life, death, or both, she closed her book of dreams and forgot about it. Not only did she stop awakening to ponder her dreams, but over time she left off dreaming altogether. There was only one problem. The meaning of her life was closed to her. Not only did she refuse to explore it, but also, ever so much sadder, she had forgotten how. As Emerson put it in one of his beautiful turns of phrase, "Having gone through all degrees, she had become case-hardened against the veracities of the Universe."

We have many tombs in which to hide. One may be sealed against the intrusion of heartbreak or pain, the price we often pay when we dream, entrusting our love to another or investing our passion in a cause. Another may be filled with noise sufficient to drown out our thoughts and anesthetize our minds.

While living in New York City, the poet W. H. Auden visited a Forty-second Street nightclub. From the vantage point of a corner table, he studied the faces of those about him. He read traces of boredom, futility, and disillusionment. Turning over the placemat on his table, he penned this poem:

> *Faces along the bar*
> *Cling to their average day:*
> *The lights must never go out.*
> *The music must always play, . . .*
> *Lest we should see where we are,*
> *Lost in a haunted wood,*
> *Children afraid of the night*
> *Who have never been happy or good.*

To die before one's time is easy. Hieroglyphs may decorate our tomb, pictures of domestic bliss from long ago, a favorite painting that we bought when we were young or some other once precious reminder. We put in live appearances—at work or in the neighborhood, on our porch, in the mall—but, save our instinct for survival, nothing really matters when we insist on spending more and more time in our tomb.

My own tomb is far from empty. In fact, passing more than the occasional hour there, I have grown rather fond of it. I'm talking not just about killing time but about refusing to risk the sting and victory, not of death but of life. I'm talking about hiding, protecting myself, relying on pattern, routine, and habit, about not feeling deeply enough for pain to sink in and joy to break through. I don't sleep in my tomb; I lie awake there. I make excuses. I say, "No, thank you," "I'm sorry," "I don't think so," "I can't," or "Not today." I keep track of statistics: stock statistics, baseball statistics, any kind of statistics. If not bad in and of itself, when indulged as a form of escape, this is still another way to practice death.

Why do I spend so much time in my tomb? Because I'm safe there, safe from disappointment and failure, above all safe from unexpected and potentially uncomfortable human encounters. Wrapped in an antiseptic shroud, I am completely safe from life.

But that's precisely the point. Death is safe, even real death. No one can hurt you any longer. You can't make any more mistakes, no matter how you happen to be dressed when you die. The phone won't ring at 4:00 in the morning; it won't ever ring at 2:00 in the afternoon. Nothing further ventured, nothing lost. The shroud goes over you, and all is calm.

Tomb dwelling can trigger active destruction as well. I think of the Hale-Bop cult, thirty-nine science fiction and internet aficionados, who, in matching clothes, killed themselves in 1997. Obsessing on the appearance of the Hale-Bop comet, they donned black sneakers and committed suicide in order to move from our planet to the heavens. They wrapped themselves in purple shrouds, turning their world into the tomb they were trying to escape.

Jim Jones did not invent religious murder-suicide a quarter century ago in Guyana. Ever since faith was born, passionate believers have thrown themselves and others into the abyss. At the end of Umberto Eco's novel *The Name of the Rose*, the greatest library in Christendom burns to the ground, torched by a monk. The "holy" man's zeal for Christ leads him to hide and finally to obliterate any evidence that might inspire sophisticated Christians to waver in their belief. As Eco himself puts it, "Because of an excess of virtue the forces of hell prevail." The world today is rife with terrorists for truth of God. This should inspire the rest of us to invest more passion in projects that serve and heal.

On the far bank of religious fundamentalism, cults offer their members assurance that life's meaning and our ultimate triumph can be ratified by revealed truth. Most fundamentalists are peace-loving people, devoted citizens, splendid neighbors. Most people

[61]

in cults tend to mind their own business; they bother no one but themselves. There are thousands of conventicles and churches in this country whose members believe that they possess the one truth but would not begin to think about killing themselves or others, or even torching libraries, to celebrate this fact. Still, as Jim Jones and the people of the purple shroud remind us, religion can be deadly. Their tombs are monuments to credulity, not monuments to faith. Those of us less sure about the meanings of life and death should be grateful that we don't have all the answers. It's a relief not to know what comet we are heading for, or what to wear when we die.

My grandmother Jean Clark's grandfather, David Burnett, was a Mormon bishop. He came to Utah with Brigham Young and moved to Idaho in the 1860s. Just before he died, Burnett wrote his will. I found it in a family album, on lined pages in a careful, cursive hand. This will had nothing to do with matters of property. It resembled the ethical wills of thirteenth- and fourteenth-century Jews: "Study the Scriptures, obey your teachers, keep the Sabbath, do not stray from the Commandments, live a studious, upright and pure life, or you will forgo my parental blessing." Written phonetically in a Scottish brogue, David Burnett's will represents a much more substantial monument for posterity than his tomb does.

Although Burnett's will is not the one I would fashion for my own children, I admire my great-great-grandfather for setting down on paper the things he held most sacred. While writing this book, I sometimes wondered whether even it might pass muster as an ethical will. But then I recognized the conceit and folly of this idea. As Thomas Jefferson said, "It is in our lives and not our words that our religion must be read." And yet, my great-great-grandfather's mission remains a worthy one. He was reminding his successors that meaning abides more surely in our relationships than in our pocketbooks.

In a way, David Burnett was sending his descendants a time capsule. I opened his a century after he died and pondered his bequest. What would you put in your own time capsule? Imagine that one hundred years from now your great-great-grandchildren or those of your closest friends gather to open your gift to them, the essence of your being, of your priorities and values. Would you put in a hundred-dollar bill? It will be more valuable then than it is today, but does it reflect your values? Would you put in a book you wrote or a simple love letter? A diamond brooch or a pressed flower? A set of moral instructions or a recurring dream? A picture of you with the president or a picture of you as a baby, your parents playing with you in the sand?

Think of five things for which you would hope to be remembered. I know it's not easy, but I'll give you a hint that works for me. Tap the present and the present past; tap moments when you are or were yourself most fully present. Start with love; end with love. Don't try to impress. Don't try to be clever. Strip off the layers of pretense, so often born of insecurity. Think about your projects. Which ones really matter? Go to the finest places within your heart. How about a cup of tears—when your father died, or when your daughter got married? Think about an embrace that while it lasted, lasted forever. Or a time when you helped a stranger who never knew your name. Or a lifetime friendship that grew with every passing year.

Our loved ones may reject, or even expose as fraudulent, the meanings we have gleaned from life. Nonetheless, the things we hold most dear, our priorities and the limits we impose on our own behavior (as well as the arbitrary limits we refuse to accept) are the most enduring part of our legacy, the treasures we have chosen to store in our boat—our lifecraft—as we prepare to cross the heavenly waters.

Before leaving the tombs and monuments of Egypt, a word about the pharaoh Akhenaton. Akhenaton's successor and half brother, Tutankhaten (under his second name, Tutankhamen) is well known, primarily because his tomb survived intact, giving us a magnificent view of its contents. Theologically, an interesting tension existed between the two men, or at least between Akhenaton's and Tutankhamen's priests.

Due to an accident of birth, a genetic flaw, Akhenaton was born with severe deformities, a large head and unnaturally protruding buttocks and thighs. As recounted by our guide, his personal life would turn the heads of those who are nostalgic for a return to simpler, more virtuous times. Akhenaton had three daughters. Nothing else about his family was anything close to normal. First, he married his eldest daughter. Then, at the age of nine, his half brother and successor, Tutankhaten, married Akhenaton's second daughter, Tutankhaten's half sister. Finally, Akhenaton's queen, Nefertiti, who dressed as a man in order to rule as the child Tutankhaten's regent after Akhenaton's death, secured her position by marrying Akhenaton's third daughter. Alternative families were not invented yesterday.

Akhenaton was also the first unitarian. Demoting all other Gods, even popular ones, to the status of mere manifestations of the one God he recognized and worshiped, Akhenaton discovered and invented monotheism. He elevated the sun God, Aton, to the status of sole divine ruler. This did not serve the priests' purposes. For them, the more gods the merrier: the more sacrifices; the more manifold people's indebtedness to them, and the more priestly assistance people would expend to fulfill their divine obligations.

During the Protestant Reformation, when Luther and Calvin forced the Catholic saints from their status as divine intermediaries, the priestly livelihood met a similar challenge. With saints disenfranchised, the business of indulgences, tickets for heaven in exchange for some saint's intercessory favor, was curbed. To avoid a like financial curse, when Akhenaton died the priests conspired to persuade his young half brother to reinstate the fallen gods. They changed the child's name to Tutankhamen, reinstating glory to the god Amen, the most popular and therefore most profitable of gods. Quickly the old polytheism demolished Akhenaton's theological dream.

Akhenaton is best remembered for his work on the God project. His dream did not die with him. Monotheism was not dead, simply postponed for another five hundred years, when the one God was rediscovered and reinvented by the Hebrews.

5. The God Project

*Nothing any theologian ever wrote about God has
helped me very much, but everything that the poets
have written about flowers, and birds, and skies,
and seas and the saviors of the race, and God—
whoever God may be—has at one time or another
reached my soul.*   —*John Haynes Holmes,
Community Church of New York*

*They are ill discoverers that think there is no land,
when they can see nothing but sea.*
                                        —*Francis Bacon,*
THE ADVANCEMENT OF LEARNING

Somewhere in northern Vermont, after driving in uncertainty, a traveler becomes convinced that he is on the wrong road. At the next village, he comes to a halt. Calling one of the villagers to his car window, he says, "Friend, I need help. I'm lost."

"Do you know where you are?" the villager asks.

"Yes," replies the traveler. "I saw the name of your village as I entered."

The villager nods his head. "Do you know where you want to go?" he asks.

"Yes," the traveler again replies, and he names his destination.

Ruminating for a moment, the villager looks back and says, "Mister, you ain't lost. You just need directions."

It's like the Wizard of Oz. Everyone had what they were looking for; they just didn't know how to find it.

[67]

Let me share a favorite story.

Rabbi Issac of Cracow had a dream. "Travel to Prague, look under the bridge, and you will find a great treasure." The first time he had this dream, he ignored it. Rabbi Issac was a practical man. He sought neither to be nor to appear foolish. Both hopes were tested when his dream continued to recur. Finally, Rabbi Issac donned his cloak and set off for Prague in search of gold. After an arduous journey, he arrived and found the bridge easily. But there was a problem. Soldiers guarded it, day and night. Rabbi Issac waited for his opening, but the changing of the guards was too efficient. At last, he gave up, cursing himself for his credulity.

As he turned to leave, one of the soldiers finally spoke, "Hey, old man, you've been hanging about here for a long time. Now you're leaving? What am I missing?"

Rabbi Issac sighed. "I had a silly dream. I thought God was talking to me in my sleep. He told me to come here. All the way from Cracow. I shouldn't have listened."

"Foolish man," the soldier replied. "I had a dream like that once, a stupid dream. God told me to go to Cracow and look up a Rabbi Issac. I would discover a great treasure buried beneath his stove. Can you believe such a thing?" Rabbi Issac tipped his cap to the soldier, returned to Cracow, and found a great treasure buried beneath his stove.

I spent a month in Australia recently, as visiting preacher of St. Michael's Church in Melbourne. It is amazing to travel halfway around the world. I went down under and was literally upside down. Yet the sky was over my head, my feet on the ground. Simple things, like the earth being round, and around it people's heads sticking up—or down—in all different directions, intrigued me immensely.

One reason to travel—and we can do this from an armchair if we

[68]

open our minds—is to vary our perspective. For me, the primary religious emotion is awe, not only the awe that follows our inability to answer the question "Why is there something instead of nothing?" but also the awe inspired by anything from a sunset to an encounter with a previously unfamiliar, almost impossible-to-imagine living creature.

Even with the understandable goal of avoiding unnecessary surprises, if you pattern your life too carefully, slowly you lose your sense of awe. I am not speaking here of the supernatural; I am speaking of the super in the natural.Australia is more than a repository for strange animals—kangaroos, dingoes, wallabies, wombats—though wombats in their humble way are quite appealing. For me, the most amazing thing about Australia, the most eye-popping thing that Carolyn and I experienced, was the Great Barrier Reef. We spent three days on Orpheus Island, a jewel in the South Pacific surrounded by an underwater forest of coral. There were 350 kinds of coral in these waters, from mighty staghorn to intricate brain coral, fascinating colonies of living creatures in every color of the rainbow and every size imaginable. New worlds opened, articulate with the munificence of the creation. Leonardo da Vinci said it better than I can, noting that human subtlety "will never devise an invention more beautiful, more simple or more direct than does nature, because in her inventions nothing is lacking, and nothing is superfluous."

My favorite new creature was the giant clam. We saw, even touched, dozens of giant clams. Some were almost two feet tall and two feet long, each planted for all but the first ten days of their entire twenty-year lifetime in a single place, their flesh a kaleidoscope of colors and patterns, electric blues, greens, and golds, truly miraculous.

It is impossible to be blasé in the presence of a giant clam. That is a blessing, not being blasé. Viewing the creation in a new light, refracted through the crystal clear water, my wife and I saw one another with new eyes. Had that giant clam been more sentient, it would have been as surprised as we, in fact amazed by these flippered and masked, magnificent and unaccountable creatures diving to touch it and then surfacing to share their awe.

My greatest revelation on this journey came at the very last moment. The most awe-inspiring thing I saw that entire month was the Manhattan skyline at midnight as our plane approached Kennedy Airport. Skyscrapers, a billion lights, this incredible living island, pulsating, daring, magnificent! How many times have I seen the same sight, only to go back to the book I was reading, hoping to complete a chapter before I landed. That is why we need to turn everything upside down every now and again: to see it with new eyes.

We have many good reasons to turn things—even our beliefs— upside down. As Lord Acton once said, "Every institution finally perishes by an excess of its own first principle." When we believe too ardently in our own first principles, we elevate them to idols. However noble, any virtue can become an idol. When we turn that which is good into an absolute, often the results are degrading. An excess of patriotism becomes jingoistic nationalism; an excess of frugality can result in meanness or miserliness; generosity can become irresponsible largesse; extreme prudence leads to passivity; absolute justice excludes mercy, and pure mercy, justice; faith can lapse into credulity, and conviction into bigotry.

Whatever project we may be pursuing, as soon as we think we have something right side up we should experiment by flipping it over. Ralph Waldo Emerson said the same thing about theology, suggesting that we constantly vary our angle of vision, even our angle on God. If you believe in God, look again at what you believe in and cast it into question. Comfortable beliefs lack the element of surprise that invokes awe. So expand your frame of vision. Suspend your belief. Your God is probably far too small to be deserving of the name. By the same token, if you doubt God's existence, the God you disbelieve in is probably even smaller. So take a chance. Suspend your disbelief.

I once decided that I was not religious, simply because I rejected the first God I was introduced to. How incredibly unimaginative, to let someone else define God for you and, then, having outgrown their definition, never to unshutter and look out a larger window.

Human history presents a pageant of Gods, one succeeding the next. Begin with the cave dwellers, for whom the greatest imaginable powers were forces of nature. Hunters and masters of fire, they heard God thundering from the heavens, electrifying the landscape with lightning bursts of anger, shaking the earth, and flushing the game from the rocks into traps they set in the valleys below. "God" was in fire, lightning, thunder, and even the game they hunted to give them sustenance.

When agriculture replaced hunting and gathering, the female metaphor of fecundity supplanted that of the male hunter and spear thrower. God became Goddess, the womb more emblematic of creation and destruction than lightning bolts or spears. Power now lay in reaping and sowing, in the turning of the seasons. Fecundity determined survival. "God" became "Goddess," procreation creation, birth life.

With the city state, power was cloaked in the robes of authority. God was now Lord and King, protector and enforcer, leader and judge. The king or lord dispensed favors, gathered a portion of each person's bounty, and led his people into battle against other kings and lords.

The Hebrews believed that their God and King was the only God and King. Their one God punished and rewarded his people not according to their allegiance but according to their behavior. This prompted a religion with ethical foundations. With God rewarding moral actions more swiftly than he did ritual sacrifices, new religious images emerged. "You are our Father," Isaiah said. Jesus spoke of God as "Abba," or Daddy. Jesus intuited that God is not only beyond us but also within us, participating in our love for others and in our quest for justice. With this our sense of closeness found even more intimate expression.

The biography of God continues through the Enlightenment, when—with our newfound ability to make a watch—the Deists' "God" turned out to be a watchmaker. He created the world, set it ticking, and then moved on to his next creation. Modern science suggests metaphors for God that arise too from recent discoveries, like the holograph, when the whole is in each of the parts, or the Gaia hypothesis, when Mother Earth reprises the Goddess in a more embracing way. Even as each organism is a colony of cells and organs are coded with the same DNA, by the same measure, everything that lives may compose a larger organism marked with the DNA of God. This is not to suggest that we are God's creator. Whether based on societal, scientific, or theological metaphors, our "inventions" of God simply suggest the possible nature of the creator.

Let me take you on a journey, not my journey, yours. Most spiritual teachers lead us down the path they themselves have followed in search of God. Especially if we share the teacher's viewpoint and temperament, such guidance can be helpful. But even as a lesson on advanced geometry would likely not enhance the artistry of an aspiring dancer, one person's instructions for approaching God may lead another to frustration. The most cursory survey of Christian saints demonstrates how many different paths there are toward

spiritual enlightenment. Forcing a young Saint Francis to follow
the steps of Saint Joan of Arc would only frustrate, not advance, his
progress, and vice versa.

None of the seven well-worn paths I invite you to consider following (or which you are already following) is superior to the next. Pro-
gressions from primitive to advanced (as in stages of growth theory,
where one level leads to the next) don't work when we search for
God. Yet, our nature, temperament, and personality do help determine our spiritual path. Every God project will be unique, but
each of the seven types does have its own distinctive nature and
approach. No search falls into one single category. You may follow
three paths farther than most people do one. On the other hand,
one way will almost surely come more naturally to you than do the
others.

A word of warning. However you design your God project, every
path to God has its pitfalls. The light that shines on every seeker
casts a shadow. For instance, the Mystic by nature may be myopic
with respect to justice, even as the Champion, whose primary virtue is justice, may struggle with love and forgiveness. Though there
are many paths to God, in my experience, these seven are the most
familiar.

The Child

Rarest of the types, the Child views all creation as enchanted. Tod-
dlers can turn anything into a toy. In the same respect, the Child
can find good, and therefore God, almost anywhere. Jesus said
that we have to become like little children to enter the Kingdom of
Heaven. He meant that many so-called adult qualities—skepti-
cism, cynicism, world-weariness, and the like—can blind us to the
heaven that is in a mustard seed, present only to the most open
and least jaundiced eye. In literature, one example of the Child as

seeker is Prince Dimitri in Dostoyevsky's *The Idiot*. Sophisticates view him as a fool, and his openness and innocence make him vulnerable to ridicule, but acting according to his nature, he proves to be almost Christlike in his actions and thoughts.

Only rarely does the Child survive childhood. Many adults who fall into this category are "retarded" or "simple." Paradoxically, the same defects that make such people unsuited to the rigors of adult society allow them to develop a spontaneous and beautiful relationship with God.

The pitfalls of this type are obvious. Even as innocence is lovely, naïveté is not. Nor are being childish and being childlike the same thing. The Child often lacks an eye for evil. But this type of seeker more than compensates for her or his shortcomings by helping the rest of us to open our eyes a little wider, wonder at the beauty of the most ordinary things, and see God in their linings.

The Lover

The Lover's path to God is through the human heart. When Jesus tells the story of the Good Samaritan or answers his disciples' questions concerning how to get to heaven by suggesting that they "feed the hungry, clothe the naked, heal the sick, and visit those in prison," he shines his light down the Lover's path.

Often the Lover sets out to search for God only after experiencing some great suffering, a failure or personal tragedy. Such a crisis can lead to despair through isolation and bitterness, but it need not. Seekers embark on the Lover's path when their own experience makes them more compassionate toward others through the empathy of shared suffering. To recognize one's own tears in another's eyes can create a human connection that is divine.

The Lover almost always finds forgiveness (which is next to godliness) to be a natural act, one that leads to self-acceptance (at its deepest level, "peace with God"). The greatest natural limitation the Lover must often be aware of is that focusing on compassion may blind him or her to questions of justice. Mercy can cloud judgment. Also, following an individualistic path to God through one-on-one relationships can distract the Lover from evils of society that demand a more prophetic response.

The Champion

Unlike the Lover, the Champion has a natural instinct for human rights in the larger, societal sense. Driven by a passion for righteousness, often fostered by a consciousness of her or his own sense of guilt (or sin), when the Champion serves, and therefore seeks, God, it is by pursuing justice. The Hebrew prophets were Champions, advocating the rights of the poor not as individuals but as a class. For such seekers, to embark on the path toward God can transform what otherwise might remain an obsession with their own sense of sin into a quest for justice.

The principle danger for Champions is that their preoccupation with righteousness may be accompanied by an insensitivity to mercy and an inability to forgive. In extreme cases the Champion can even become a terrorist for God. On the other hand, throughout history almost every triumph of social justice has been powered by the conviction of Champions. If at times it may be said that Champions "love humankind, it is only human beings they can't stand," Champions who remain mindful of the other paths to God, and thus temper their natural passion for justice with an appreciation for mercy, become soldiers for good and pillars of faith.

The Servant

The Servant follows the most traditional path to God, relying on the authority of scripture, following the teachings of religious

authorities, and joining together with others in religious fellow-
ship. Servants receive guidance from many generations of teachers,
find truth and meaning in the great religious writings, and give positive reinforcement to those who walk down the same path, as well
as receiving it from them. Because of the richness of scripture and
the insight of spiritual guides who draw from the same material,
the Servant draws from a long and proven tradition to help discover his or her way.

Servants seek and find authority outside of themselves. Their
goal is truth, which they are taught, and believe, is codified in the
scriptures. When they follow a broad way, they and others are safe,
even more than safe. The danger comes when Servants are led
down a false path by false teachers. Servants can have so narrow a
view of truth that they deem others who follow different paths to
be headed not toward a different view of illumination but toward
damnation.

Fortunately, the great religious traditions are by nature self-
correcting, and Servants often are able to follow both their own
nature and the teachings of authorities toward an ever deeper
appreciation for God.

The Dreamer

Dreamers are mythmakers. Rather than discovering God within
ordinary experience (whether heaven in a wildflower, a scripture,
an act of justice, or an act of love), Dreamers project their experience of reality onto a cosmic screen, creating a heavenly drama of
mythic proportion. Dreamers draw more on imagination than experience. They invent rather than discover God. Not that what they
invent is unreal. Given the mystery of God's nature, Dreamers may
come closer to certain aspects of God's nature through their vivid
imaginations than do others through their experience of common

reality. Every creation myth and Armageddon scenario, even those contained in scripture, is spun from Dreamers' speculation. Dreamers think big. Though often impelled by fears of things unseen, they find hope by spinning fantasies that give portent and meaning to life.

The Dreamer's virtue is hope. A world exists beyond the seen world, giving meaning to what otherwise might seem to make no apparent sense, especially death. The pitfall here is that Dreamers may supplant reality with fantasy, deprecating the value of the all-too-human in their search for the mythic underpinnings of reality. When they lose themselves in their thoughts, Dreamers create a world that no one else actually inhabits. Like conspiracy theorists, they create a hyperrational reality, one that has no basis in our shared experience. Yet, Dreamers also paint on a larger canvas than do most people, and thus they give more expression to the drama and majesty of creation. Looking down at our paths in order not to make a misstep, the rest of us may completely miss what Dreamers see.

The Mystic

The Mystic is the most introverted and attentive of God's seekers. By nature a loner, or by some stroke of fate driven toward solitude for solace, the Mystic seeks illumination through long stretches of quiet contemplation. Solitude and loneliness are different things. Solitude is the fullness, loneliness the emptiness, of being alone. Some Mystics, more gregarious by nature, draw on personal powers of intuition or healing to minister directly to others. In either case, the path to God involves self-emptying. Mystics aspire to become open vessels for the Holy Spirit.

More intimate than any other path, the Mystic's illumination comes in a passive form. Every faith contains mystic exemplars, most of whom would relate more empathetically to mystics of other religions than to nonmystical members of their own. The greatest danger of contemplative mysticism is that Mystics withdraw, even from their own human needs, to make room for God. Conversely, Mystics who are healers or diviners can confuse their own power with God's, and thereby become dangerous to the people who turn to them for help. Charlatans can ape the Mystics' insight and do harm to the credulous, but most Mystics need only take care not to delude themselves. Their gift of self-emptying, which is both rare and special enough to be honored and cherished, gives Mystics a special place among God's seekers.

The Star Gazer

The Star Gazer divines God in cosmic details. Unlike Dreamers, whose approach is Mythic, Star Gazers respond to the mystery of the creation with a different kind of awe. Drawing from experience, Dreamers project divine figures onto a cosmic screen; Star Gazers ponder the universe to discover hints of cosmic purpose. Their virtue is humility. With 200 billion stars in our galaxy and as many as 100 billion galaxies, Star Gazers sit on the very edge of the universe. They ponder bigger things than can be imagined. Many great scientists, ancient and modern, are Star Gazers. As one cosmologist said, "The universe is not only queerer than we imagined, it's queerer than can be imagined." Humility invites the Star Gazer to embrace all others as one, mysteriously born, fated to die, children of creation, seeds of a divine mystery.

That this is by far the widest-ranging path to God is precisely the Star Gazer's problem. God can become an abstraction, a great oblong blur. What fascinates the human mind may not touch the human heart. When we mortals are in pain, infinity can be cold, unresponsive, even merciless. On the other hand, awe and humility constitute our most primal human religious response. Any path to God that can lead to each of these in such profound measure is a true and worthy one.

The God project need not necessarily have God as its object. Call God "Truth," "Ultimate Reality," the "Ground of Being," or anything you wish. The word "God" is nothing more (or less) than a sign pointing to an ultimate reality that finally can be neither named nor known.

Whichever path you follow, in your search for God you will never finally discover what you seek. God is far too mysterious and multifaceted for any of us to comprehend. Ultimate goals will always prove elusive. On the other hand, on the road to God, we may find ourselves. Even here we must be careful. The closer we get to the light, the longer a shadow we may cast.

Let me close with a parable, offered (with apologies) in the manner of Plato. We are standing in the middle of a circle, the circumference of which contains all the possibilities of life. God (or Ultimate Reality) is outside the circumference of our circle shining in from all directions. One person can journey to the right and another to the left. If each travels the same distance during his or her lifetime, although searching for meaning in opposite directions, they will end up equally close to the light. Yet one will be more enlightened than the other. How can this be? If not apparent from the light shining on their faces, the reason is simple.

Let's say that one of these two pilgrims, knowing that he is approaching the light, believes that the light lies only in his direction, shining on his face and no one else's. Since belief in this world (as in ours) affects reality, his light will cast a long, dark shadow. Should he lack empathetic imagination, by blocking out the light shining from any direction other than the one he is facing, the closer he gets to the circumference of the circle, and therefore to the light, the longer and darker will be the shadow that he casts.

Let's say that the second pilgrim, approaching the same light while going in the opposite direction, knows or senses that the light shines from every point outside the circle—from behind her as well as in front of her. This belief permits the light shining on other people's faces to reduce her shadow. No closer to the light, is not she more enlightened than the man who casts the shadow?

One further question: Why does she continue in this direction, if other paths might serve her as well as the one she has chosen? Perhaps because she knows that she can go farther toward the light by following a single path than by walking around in circles and taking day hikes on every path that meets her fancy.

To my Platonic parable, let me add another question. To find God, does the pilgrim necessarily have to travel anywhere? After all, the treasure she seeks may be buried beneath her stove.

6. The Music of Prayer

Harpists spend half their life tuning and the other half
playing out of tune.   *—Anonymous*

Take but degree away, untune that string,
And, hark! What discord follows.
                    —William Shakespeare, THE TEMPEST

Several years ago my wife, Carolyn, and I traveled to Davos, Switzerland, where she served as a delegate to the World Economic Forum. Throughout the week, as a fly on the wall, I marveled at the commitment and intelligence of the world leaders who gathered there. My favorite encounter took place on the way back from Davos to Geneva to catch the plane home. Our driver overheard me recounting a dream to Carolyn that identified me as a minister. This prompted an hourlong monologue that was colorful, irreverent, and passionate, a pastiche of free association that we audited with growing appreciation and amusement. You can learn something about prayer anywhere, even on a taxi ride.

In Switzerland, the church is underwritten by the government. An established church supported by taxes—exactly the opposite of how religious charitable giving works in the United States. Here members of specific congregations contribute what they choose or can to their own church or synagogue. In Switzerland everyone who gives tithes through a government assessment. If you have moral—namely antireligious grounds—not to do this, you file a claim and your taxes are reduced. No wonder there are fewer Swiss Christians on the books every year.

Our driver turned out to be what might best be described as a large-hearted skeptic. He couldn't buy orthodox theology, but he did believe in many of the good works that various churches sponsored. He paid his religious tax, but not passively. Having contributed to the general fund, this character decided that he was a stakeholder. I can assure you, this particular gadfly is never outside the room.

He attended a church concert where the minister's wife was one of the soloists and his son a principal accompanist. According to our source, the minister could not lavish too much praise on his loved ones, even as he neglected thanking all the other singers and accompanists. Offended, our driver called the minister at home. This holy man evidently responded in what might most generously be called irreligious language (I sympathize; it may have been late). Our good citizen then called the president of the congregation. When the president sidestepped him, he went directly to the press. His letter to the editor and subsequent meetings between the minister, his family, the president, and the good citizen led to a public apology. Our driver said that his concern was for the other children, who needed all the positive reinforcement they could receive if they were to develop sufficient self-esteem to have—and these were his exact words—"enough left over as adults to give something to others, as Jesus said."

One Christmas Eve, our universal Christian read in the paper that

an unconventional clergyman was about to be fired for behavior
unbefitting a minister. As a stakeholder, he decided to check the situation out for himself. He sacrificed part of his preferred celestial
concert and dropped by the church in question. Its foyer was filled
with barn animals. The minister, dressed in lederhosen, moved
back and forth between this makeshift crèche and seventy homeless
people, whom, in the true Christmas spirit, his church was feed-
ing. "The man was a little weird," our driver said, "but so was
Jesus." As a taxpayer who believed that he should have some say
about who his ministers were, he hit the press again. After a two-
week mini-tempest, with the minister, taxi driver, and sheep promi-
nently featured on local television, the pastor was given back his
job.

One hundred fifty years ago, the Christian existentialist philosopher Søren Kierkegaard, a brooding loner with an incisive mind,
differentiated between the practice of Christianity and the state of
Christendom. As he saw it, in his own country, Denmark, and
throughout Europe, while Christendom was reigning triumphant,
Christianity was dead. "Christendom," he wrote, "openly or more
hiddenly, now by attack, now by defense, has abolished Christianity." In Kierkegaard's view, the Christian establishment had
become so completely co-opted by secularity and the gospel of comfort, success, and the status quo, that Christianity, namely the gospel of Jesus, was stifled wherever it might dare to emerge in plain
view. Turning signposts into hitching posts, Christians had
become idolaters.

In the early twentieth century, the philosopher Henri Bergson
expanded a like critique into the major thesis of his book *The Two
Sources of Morality and Religion*. Bergson speaks of static and
dynamic religion. Each religion or system of morality goes through

[83]

natural stages of growth. The aperture of vision and spiritual adventure opens and closes in succession over time, resulting in periods that can be described, respectively, as dynamic and static.

Beginning with the Jews, a dynamic stage commences in the seventh and eighth centuries B.C.E. with the emergence of the prophets. With their chastening critique of society, such figures as Jeremiah, Hosea, Amos, and Ezekiel revitalized the Hebrew faith. They were idol smashers. At the close of this period, new prophecy was outlawed and the writings of the prophets were frozen into pillars of the temple establishment. A new dynamic stage is triggered by the teachings of Jesus of Nazareth, who exacted liberty from the letter of the law by invoking the spirit that originally informed it. He overturned the tables of the money changers in the temple, and the wildfire of a new gospel blazed throughout the Mediterranean world. A static stage follows as the church is established as a power unto itself. With the conversion of Constantine in 313 C.E., the state is brought in as a steward or co-regent of the church. By this time the perimeters for heresy have been drawn so tightly that even Jesus likely would have been excluded from the fold. Luther and Calvin ushered in another dynamic period during the Protestant Reformation, when the teaching authority as well as the moral authority of Rome was placed in question and a radical new principle, that of *Sola Scriptura* (by scripture alone), reawakened Europe, giving the spirit new power and renewed life.

I am simplifying Bergson's thesis. Throughout those periods in which religion has been static, groups and individuals have rallied to the power of the Holy Spirit. Nothing of human keeping is ever pure from adulteration. The dynamic can become demonic, even as the static can preserve institutions and values of unquestionable worth. Yet idolatry invades our churches and other ongoing institutions when they serve as little more than sanctuaries for those who

[84]

wish to take refuge from the present in the past. This is the very definition of static religion: self-absorbed, self-protective, and ultimately, where it matters most, within our very souls, self-destructive. Churchgoers are particularly vulnerable because association with a religious institution can lead to a sense of moral superiority. This is as true of my own church as any other. Every religious institution embodies the almost inevitable pretense that God—love and justice, the spirit of life, or whatever we most highly value there—is ensconced within its walls, happily receiving our ministrations and grateful for our goodness and generosity in offering them.

Precisely the opposite may be true. To the extent that we believe ourselves better than others because we are religious, we insulate ourselves from our common humanity. We forget that we are all wandering in a vast and impenetrable wilderness. Religious institutions have always competed for greatness and superiority. If God decides to take a taxi ride on Sunday rather than go to church, this may be why.

Our Swiss cabdriver was definitely Kierkegaardian. With a keen eye for idolatry, he loved Christianity and disdained Christendom. But he was also Bergsonian. He sought to enliven his own faith with a more dynamic dimension. As it turns out, what he really wanted to talk to us about was prayer. Changing his tone entirely, he raised what he called "a serious religious question"—one he answered for himself in the following monologue.

"I don't know about you," the driver said, "but I have trouble with the Lord's Prayer. I believe in God, but the Lord's Prayer, I mean, since I say it every night before I go to bed, I had to improve on it, I just had to. What's this 'Our Father' business. If God's a man, we're finished. And how about 'Who art in heaven.' Wait a minute, all of us are here, so what I say is this: 'Holy Spirit, who art with and among us,' and then I drop the bit about the hallowed name, because that doesn't mean anything.

" 'Thy Kingdom come, thy will be done,' same problem. I say 'Be with us as we would be with you.' Then, 'give us this day our daily bread.' That didn't make sense to me, until I heard a sermon once. I didn't like the preacher, but it was a good sermon; it got me thinking. We're not talking about hamburgers here; we're talking about spiritual food, the stuff that makes us human. So I left that in.

"As for 'Forgive us our trespasses as we forgive those who trespass against us,' just talk to my girlfriend. I had to leave that in. But this 'Lead us not into temptation and deliver us from evil' business. Give me a break. What's the deal? We ask God not to lead us into temptation, and then, when bad things happen even when we've been good, blame God for it? That's ridiculous. I dropped that out.

"Which leaves only 'Thine is the power and the glory for ever and ever, Amen.' I have no real problem with that but it doesn't really do much for me. So I say, 'Thank you for the blessing of life. I pray I may be worthy of it.' Believe me, it sounds better in German."

It doesn't sound bad in English:

> *Holy Spirit, who art with and among us,*
> *Be with us as we would be with you,*
> *Give us this day our daily bread,*
> *Forgive us our trespasses as we forgive those who*
> *trespass against us.*
> *Thank you for the blessing of life,*
> *I pray I may be worthy of it.*

"The last line's the hard one," he said. "I'm not part of a church, but I support good works. That's one piece of it. Now I've got to do my bit to throw my body where my money is. This year I have.

Maybe I'll start going to church, try to find one that works. Tell me about yours."

Slightly trepidatious that he might show up next Christmas Eve and complain to the press about my mentioning Carolyn in the sermon or a lack of homeless people in the vestibule, I took him on my five-minute tour of Unitarianism. He replied that this seemed just about as good as all the rest of them. He'd drop by one day when he next came to New York.

This man inspired me. A skeptic, he had as much passion and as deeply cultivated a set of convictions as any true believer. He knew and acknowledged his own faults. He owed something to society and didn't begrudge paying for it. He cared deeply about important things: equity, social service, and God. He worked on his own faith daily to fashion a set of principles he could live by. And he said his prayers.

Do you say your prayers? You should. It is a splendid project, one of the best ways I know to discover and create meaning. No special expertise is involved. You can have as free a spirit as my Swiss cabdriver and still say your prayers.

It happens in the strangest of places. Even in a taxi with a silent driver. You can fret over found time and watch it slip through your glass. Run in place and time will slip away. But one of these days you may forget to run. When this happens, just perhaps, you may find yourself suspended in the mystery of prayer.

For me, it starts as meditation. There is nothing to be done, so I do nothing. When I empty myself of frets, worries, preoccupations, and distractions, quite unexpectedly I am filled by the spirit of God. It never lasts for long. Before I know it, I am off and running once again. Besides, it is difficult to credit any experience, however affecting, when it happens in so unlikely a place as a taxi.

[87]

If there is a God, you would expect to encounter God on a mountaintop. The problem is, how many mountaintops do we visit in any given lifetime? Not that many. And when we finally do get to the mountaintop, often we are disappointed. Clouds block our view. It is cold. Other mountains come into range, great and distant, that either we must climb or we know we never shall. As for the taxi stand, it is just around the corner, but so is God.

This is the message of Jesus. And not only as recorded in the familiar places. Fifty years ago a little book of sayings attributed to Jesus, the Gospel of Thomas, was unearthed in the sands of Egypt. In it Jesus' disciples ask him when the Realm of God is going to come. "What you expect has come," Jesus replies, "but you know it not."

As meaning-seekers often do, by running after God, Jesus' disciples escaped being caught by God. Think of that fateful night in the Garden at Gethsemane. Perhaps it was because they had been running so hard that, exhausted, their eyes grew heavy and they drifted off to sleep while Jesus prayed. But at least they knew to ask the right question: "When is the realm of God going to come?" Much of the time we are too preoccupied with lesser pursuits to do even that. I can hear Jesus saying (as he does in the Gospel of Thomas), "What deep within your hearts you truly seek has come, but you expect it not."

We live in an amazing age. Conveniences are many, and entertainments, more alluring than ever, are accessible in unprecedented quantity and variety: television, video games, sports, liquor, drugs, the stimuli that captivate our minds, all of it packaged attractively for every pocketbook and taste. How easily and comfortably we are swept along. The lowest common denominator veritably sparkles. Inertia leads, and we follow in the dance.

Most of us manage to make a working pact with life. We settle into routines, cope surprisingly well with hardship, rise to occasions, and wend our way more or less successfully from one day to the next. I am no exception. My life is ever so much more pleasant than unpleasant, far more rewarding than it is taxing. I enjoy my little triumphs. I savor moments of relaxation with my family and friends. And yet, I take so much for granted: my loved ones, my projects, life itself. What is more, I begrudge these things the difficulties they cause me. I forget how much they mean to me. How much they simply mean.

I fill my days. There are things to be done and things to be avoided. We each have our race to run with time. Not that this is always bad, but lacking something more, the meaning piece is missing. Most of us know this. The question is, what, if anything, are we prepared to do about it?

One thing we can do is to say our prayers. If difficult to sustain, saying our prayers is not that hard a project to begin. Take ten minutes here or twenty minutes there. Once or twice a day, simply stop running. When you intentionally stop running, prayer begins.

It is eleven o'clock in the evening. The children are in bed. I am sitting on the couch in my living room. I must be tired. I am distracted, preoccupied by the day's events. My mind is racing, getting nowhere. It covers a little ground, then circles back, half attentive, locked into fresh ruts. Or it stops somewhere and spins. Vagrant images, many of them painful, steal into my consciousness. How readily we submit to reliving the same disappointment over and over again. "I should have said. . . . I wish I had. . . . Of course, he didn't give me half a chance. . . . but, even so, I should have said. . . ." Nothing earth-shattering, just the usual mix of unprocessed emotions, haunting memories, and nagging thoughts, the old familiar ever-unfinished business of the mind.

And then I remember to stop. I disengage the wheels that grind and spin. I take one deep breath, and then another. The ground of my being firms. I feel for a center that will hold me, and I yield.

With prayer, beginning is the most difficult, to stop running and spinning, intentionally to yield. It is hard to let go of anything that is ours, even things that sting or wound when we refuse to let them go. Anger. Embarrassment. Bitterness. Envy. Even things we hate. We hoard them like treasures. They litter our minds. The way we cherish our grievances and mistakes, you'd think they were the most holy thing in our lives.

Have you ever stopped to notice how people tend to flaunt their resentments almost as if they were a matter of great pride? "How are you?" we ask. "Oh," they reply, in a manner more expressive of smugness than resignation, "you don't really want to know." They do want us to know, of course, for there is no higher privilege than to be numbered among life's choir of victims. This is a choir unlike any other. It is a choir in name only. Every voice in it is a solo voice. Each sings his or her own sad music, oblivious to or even scornful of the human chorus welling through the loft.

Most of us are not that hard-bitten. Even so, human nature makes us reluctant to cede our little place of privilege in the choir. Whenever we are inclined to feel sorry for ourselves or to indulge in self-flagellation, there is a ready part for us. We close our eyes, stop our ears, and sing.

Prayer is the opposite. Even before it is an act of self-expression, prayer is an act of empathy. Prayer involves listening. In fact, it is the discipline of listening. Discipline and prayer mean much the same thing. The Latin root for discipline means to listen. A disciple is one who listens; we listen when we pray. And simply by listening, how much we gain. From broken melody we move to harmony; we resolve our dissonance into consonance; we tune our voices to the key of the cosmos.

To keep ourselves halfway decently in tune, we must tinker all the time. Here on our anger. There on our bitterness or lethargy, our pettiness or pride. Fully to love, we must mute our fears. To serve, we must tone down our piping little egos. In order to produce anything like beautiful music, we must join in the human band, march with and for them, be an instrument of their peace.

Prayer is one proven way to keep in tune. First, it is a means by which we can keep in tune with ourselves; it shapes and colors our melody. Prayer also helps us stay in tune with others; it brings us into harmony. Finally, prayer tunes us to the cosmos, to the overarching and all-sustaining spirit of life; it recalls us to the symphony.

There are three fundamental kinds of relationships. Prayer speaks to each of them. The first is internal, one's relationship with oneself. A prayer of confession, with a pledge to change, can promote self-honesty and therefore integrity, or wholeness. The second is external, one's relationships with others. Prayers of petition, of intercession or forgiveness, can bring us closer to others, even those from whom we are estranged. The third kind of prayer is both internal and external. It relates to life, to the animating power of being. Prayers of thanksgiving or consecration connect us to the Holy.

The words *wholeness, health,* and *holy* each share the same Teutonic root. In Latin, salvation also means health or wholeness. If divided within ourselves, estranged from others, or alienated from the ground of our being, we are not whole but broken. Prayer saves us. It helps heal our brokenness.

But first we must acknowledge that we are broken. This is hard. We are so busy trying to hold ourselves together that we can find precious little time in any given day to contemplate our brokenness. Again, it's a matter of project management. How much easier it is to run and hide, or simply to keep on going as we are—not so good, not so bad—until the sand runs out of our glass. Prayer says stop. Winnow out distractions. Come to attention. Catch your breath. Gather your resources. Listen. If we are too busy to spend twenty minutes a day doing this, something is wrong.

Taking the time is no small accomplishment. Find twenty minutes in the morning or evening uninterrupted, spent in a quiet place, and you are halfway there. Focus your mind, gather your strength, and ready yourself for the miracle of another day or night. If you do nothing with this time other than consciously and deliberately listen to your heart beat and feel the life within, you will have accomplished a great deal. This is what most forms of meditation are about. Get comfortable, breathe deeply, relax. Prayer need have no object beyond this. Meditation tunes the soul, and wholeness can follow.

Directed prayer is more complex. The goal of confession is integrity (the honest confrontation with ourselves as we are); the goal of petition, at least in its higher forms, is reconciliation (the acceptance and forgiveness of others as they are); and the goal of thanksgiving, or consecration, is holiness (the emptying of ourselves that we may be filled with God). In directed prayer we seek integrity in place of disintegration, reconciliation in place of estrangement, and holiness in place of fragmentation. Each is a metaphor for wholeness.

I know that I am preaching here, even a bit schematically. You cannot expect to pick up a book by a preacher that doesn't have at least a little bit of preaching in it. So let me give you one more hint about the hardest kind of prayer, prayers of forgiveness.

Picture in your mind the face of someone from whom you are estranged. Pray for them. You will discover that it is impossible to hate someone and pray for them at the same time. This may not change her or his attitude toward you, but it may lift at least some of the burden of resentment you carry in your own heart.

The English poet George Herbert once wrote, "He who cannot forgive others destroys the bridge over which he himself must pass." In a like sense, when we reconcile ourselves with another, we ourselves are healed; a bridge is built from estrangement to wholeness over which we then can cross. Our love too can then cross the desert self that lies between where we are and who we might be. This is the forgiveness project. Its potential for meaning will surprise both others and us.

Forgiveness is not easy. If it didn't matter so much, we might justify a life of watching bridges burn, or squeezing solace from a desert cactus. Such a life can be lived, but not justified. No amount of self-righteousness, self-justification, or self-pity will turn the trick. To be at enmity with life is to bleed life of meaning, and to be at enmity with another is to be at enmity with life. This is why Jesus told his disciples to love and pray for their enemies. No peace in the world surpasses the peace of a forgiving and self-accepting heart. We cannot control our destiny or what others will think of us or do to us. But we do have power over how we respond.

Nothing I have said about prayer will lay to rest the doubts of a skeptic. To one who refuses to pray, prayer will remain foreign, suspicious, and strange. But, in the spirit of William James's "will to believe" and that of my Swiss cabdriver, I can promise you, prayer can be self-ratifying in the life of those who dare to pray. The rest remains with God.

7. A Mystery Story

*The fairest thing we can experience is the mysterious.
It is the fundamental emotion which stands at the
cradle of true science. He who knows it not, and can no
longer wonder, no longer feel amazement, is as good as
dead. We all had this priceless talent when we were
young. But as time goes by, many of us lose it. The true
scientist never loses the faculty of amazement. It is the
essence of his being.*

—Hans Selye, NEWSWEEK, *1958*

*All things cover up the same mystery; all things are
veils that cover God.*

—Pascal, PENSÉES

Begin at the beginning. Where did we come from, and why did we
turn up when and where we did? Choice may be a factor during the
course of our lives, but it had nothing to do with our arriving here
in the first place. We didn't choose our parents. We didn't choose
our country. We didn't choose the economic stratum into which we
were born, our gender, sexual preference, or even our century.
Again, whenever we are tempted to ask, "What did I do to deserve
this?" the answer is "Nothing." We did nothing to be here. We are
the innocent victims and unworthy beneficiaries of life's incredible
largesse.

Think back beyond your parents and grandparents, and then
back further. Think back a thousand generations. If our closest
ancestors have populated this planet for a million years, we have to
go back fifty thousand generations just to trace human ancestry. For

each of us, an almost unimaginable number of human predecessors survived infant mortality, plague, famine, and a myriad of other hardships simply to get to puberty and make love. And then, every single time, the unique sperm of millions that had us somewhere deep in its genetic pocket somehow made it to the equally unique egg.

Reckon the odds. That we should even exist staggers the imagination. Then take it back further, back to the ur-paramecium. All of us are connected genetically to the beginning of life and kinetically to the beginning of time. The universe was pregnant with us when it was born. I find this far more amazing and inspiring than most theological reflections. Simply being here—my having written, your reading—is a miracle. Consider my awe at the underwater world on the Great Barrier Reef, how impossible it was to be blasé in the presence of a giant clam. We should never be blasé when reflecting on the creation or our place in it. As it is written in the thirtieth chapter of the Book of Proverbs,

> *Three things are too wonderful for me;*
> *four I do not understand:*
> *the way of an eagle in the sky,*
> *the way of a snake on a rock,*
> *the way of a ship on the high seas,*
> *and the way of a man with a woman.*

Physics, anatomy, biology, and psychology can begin to decode such mysteries. Yet knowledge has its limits. Quoting an academic study, novelist Saul Bellow observed "that on an average weekday the *New York Times* contains more information than any contemporary of Shakespeare would have acquired in a lifetime." That includes Shakespeare himself. The *Times* is a fine paper. I read it every day. But for all its information, it only hints, and then only occasionally, at what Shakespeare knew so very well: that the beauty of the bird, the symbol of the snake, the courage of the pilot, and the wonder of human love will always be touched by mystery.

We don't need something unnatural—like a virgin birth or the stopping of the sun—to prove our faith. Neither do we need a gigabyte of data to disprove it. Beyond all proof or disproof, we need only reverence for life itself. Contemplate our awe-inspiring connection, over millennia, to thousands of human ancestors, and ultimately, to everything that lives.

One of my favorite twentieth-century theologians is Rudolph Otto. Much of what he had to say was only half intelligible. That's okay. Anyone who dares hang up a shingle as a theologian is lucky to be intelligible at all. But when identifying the core experience of religion, Otto was spot on. He described the holy as a *mysterium tremens et fascinans:* a tremendous—which means awe- and fear-inspiring—and fascinating mystery.

Consider the cosmos. There are billions of stars in our galaxy, and ours is one of perhaps 100 billion galaxies. That is only our cosmos. There could be others. Astronomers suggest that there are 200 billion stars in our galaxy alone. Each of us living on the earth today is therefore the proud possessor of twenty-five personal stars. If you choose to name yours (actually a fun thing to do), you can't start too soon. Naming one's own stars is more than a lifelong project. With 100 billion galaxies, the cosmic star to person ratio is 2.5 trillion stars to one.

So what do we do? Do we name our stars and shake our heads in wonder? No. We sit on a single grain of sand on this vast cosmic beach and argue over which religious teacher has the best insider information on God and the afterlife. Is it Jesus? Is it the Buddha? Is it Mohammed? How about Nietzsche, Einstein, or Freud? All I

[97]

know is this: Billions of accidents conspired to give each one of these compelling teachers the opportunity even to teach. Knowing this doesn't strip me of my faith. It inspires my faith. It makes me humble. It fills me with awe.

With their original font in the Hebrew scriptures, Islamic, Christian, and Jewish traditions trace our ancestry back to the Garden of Eden, to Eve and Adam, our ur-parents. As myth, this rings true to me. Not true enough, not nearly vast enough for the earth, not to mention the cosmos, but true in the sense in which it was originally intended, in the mythic sense. Creation myths remind us that we spring from the same source.

Not that we should obsess on our ancestors. Stemming from the same roots in Genesis as do the Jews, Christians, and Muslims, the Mormons place special emphasis on genealogy. They believe that if we trace our ancestries back far enough—given that anyone who was born before the nineteenth century would not have been privy to Joseph Smith's revelation—we can pray for our ancestors and liberate them from limbo.

There are limits to this scheme of redemption. Even the finest Mormon genealogist, working with the best-connected families, can make it back only to the eighth century. Those of our ancestors—and all of us had them—who were alive two, ten, or twenty thousand years ago and more are therefore toast.

In the late 1950s, shortly after my father was elected to the U.S. Senate, in a self-seeking but nonetheless generous gesture, the Mormon Church offered to do his genealogy. My mother still has it, two large vellum-covered books a thousand pages long. By dint of this exercise, I learned that I was related to Charlemagne, who evidently had numerous illegitimate children. The Mormons made only one mistake, but it was a significant mistake (in gold print on the cover of both folios). They misspelled my father's middle name, diminishing the authority of their work.

If not as important as the Mormons may think, ancestral lines do have value. They connect us intimately to the source of our being. Yet other lines may help us recognize our interdependencies even better than our bloodlines do.

I discovered this in Australia while studying the Aboriginal peoples. Aborigines—or, as they call themselves, Koories—are born into two families. The first is their blood family, and the second is their dream family, the family that places them in a larger mythos. Each dream family has not a bloodline but a songline, one connected to the natural world, each possessing its own story, a myth that is a song.

Talk about projects conducive to meaning. This one tops my list. When Koories go on what they call a walkabout—which can last for weeks—they enter the outback and follow their song. Each hill and rivulet is part of their story, a story passed down for thousands of years within each dreaming, or mythic, family. These songlines are guarded closely, but they can be traded to ensure safe passage through what might seem to the untutored eye a barren, undistinguished wilderness. There are the mosquito dreaming and the wallaby dreaming, the two babies dreaming and the butterfly dreaming, each not only a song but also a path, sometimes stretching across the vast expanse of Australia from sea to sea. Each dreaming participates in an age-old mythic drama. Also the relationship between people extends intimately to the creation itself. This is why the Koories hold their land to be sacred. If miners level hills that make up part of their story, the songline is broken.

The myths on which we base Western religion are also dreamings, but we have abstracted our songlines from the ground of our being. We divide creature from creation, relegating the world to a charnel house from which we must be saved. Here we can learn something from the ancient Koories. According to their understanding, our world is enchanted, riddled with meanings, itself sacred ground.

However far removed from the primitive mythic thought patterns of the Aborigines (far too removed to recapture our own songlines), we can certainly extend our theological imaginations beyond the dualistic Western mythos we have inherited. Think of our culture lines as songlines, a long dreaming, an ancient and continuing journey leading from the beginning of time until now. Imagine each culture line as a melody we pass along, to which succeeding generations add their voices, coupling songs, adding instruments and orchestration, building toward if not a cosmic then surely an earth-centered symphony, cacophonous but susceptible, in moments of grace, to harmonic resolution.

As a substitution for God, certain scientists speak of the evolution of memes, patterns of behavior and thinking propagated and modified by cultures. Richard Dawkins (who coined the word *meme*) offers the following examples: "tunes, ideas, catch-phrases, clothes fashions, ways of making pots or of building arches." Memes are icons we invent that catch on and then carry themselves from one generation to the next.

I have no problem with the idea of memes. Neither do I worry about memes being "viruses of the mind" or building blocks for myth. In my model for meaning, it doesn't matter. When fundamentalists, with no interest in memes, say that the scriptures are not myth but fact, and certain secular materialists, reducing the scriptures to mere memes, say they are not fact but myth, I answer both with the same question: "What's wrong with myth?" Myth is not only the language of mystery but human experience projected onto a cosmic screen. Little experiences will be dimmed by the stars, even as great ones are reflected in them. The question we should ask ourselves is whether our myth is big enough. Can it encompass the mystery, majesty, and wonder of being?

Even secular humanists cannot dismiss mystery. Bertrand Russell wrote, "It is a strange mystery that nature, omnipotent but blind, in the revolution of her secular hurryings though the abysses of space has brought forth at last a child, subject to her power, but gifted with sight and knowledge of good and evil, with the capacity of judging all the works of his unthinking mother." This is a mystical statement. It suggests that although God can be doubted, mystery still reigns.

In parsing meaning from mystery, Russell's English contemporary Burnet H. Streeter does a far better job. "The picture of the physical universe which it is the goal of science to give us is related to Reality much as an ordinance map is related to the country which it represents," he writes. "The map is absolutely correct; and to one planning a motor-tour, it is indispensable. From it we can derive the kind of knowledge which is power. I can sit in my room in Oxford and plan a motor tour through Japan. But the map is not Japan. It is precisely in the beauty of the landscape and other things in Japan which no map can represent that alone would make the motor-tour worthwhile." This point is simple and profound. Those who dissect life without appreciating the beauty and mystery that imbue it with value search for meaning where meaning can't be discovered. Much of life's meaning is numinous and, therefore, magnificently illusive.

Consider the following religious experiment, one I read about in seminary. The setting was a room, empty save for a single carpet, a cushion to sit on, and a blue vase. The project director asked a group of his students to drop by the room one at a time, morning and evening, to meditate on the vase. On emerging, they were to write down their reflections.

At the first sitting, the comments were descriptive of form and function. "I followed the contours of the vase," one person said. Another imagined it with almond blossoms in it, picturing it as a container, to which the director replied, "Don't do that sort of thing; there's far too much thinking going on here; just meditate as it were on the vasishness of the vase."

After these mystifying instructions, they returned the next day and tried again. Over time, the students reported deeper spiritual encounters. "I felt as if the vase and I were one," or "I seemed to merge into the vase," some rhapsodically exclaimed. With each sitting, their religious experience heightened. At the end of the week, the director removed the vase from the room. The students arrived as usual. On entering they discovered that the vase was gone. Many were stunned by a feeling of loss.

"Where is the vase?" they asked.

"Surely you don't need the vase now?" the director replied.

Shortly after my father died, I wrote a statement of faith. Struggling with loss and death, I grounded it in mystery. Over the years my theology has developed, but my faith remains much as it was then. Together with humility and awe, my through lines are love and death.

Growing up, I believed in God without questioning what I meant. God was God, and that was that. At the age of three, my daughter had reached about the same level of theological sophistication that I achieved at a somewhat less precocious age. You'd ask her where God lives. She'd point to the sky and go on with her business.

For me, more important than the existence of God was that of the goblins and evil spirits that lurked under my bed at night. About them I knew at least this much. When my mother turned on the light, got on her hands and knees, raised the bedspread, and looked under the bed, they were gone. When she turned off the light and left the room, they returned in force to haunt me.

In my early years, God figured in precisely the opposite fashion. When things were going well, when I did not need God, God was there. I believed in God without worrying about why. When darkness fell and I was troubled, when I experienced what in later years would recur periodically as a dark night of the soul, I could not sense God anywhere.

If God did exist, God was not important to me. I believed in what I could see, touch, learn, and love. Compared to these, the wonders of a distant God in heaven held no allure. I found myself believing in the rainbow, but not in the pot of gold at the end of it. If such a thing existed, it was not important to me. More precisely, I knew enough, or thought I did, not to search for the rainbow's end, for such a search would be vain. By the time I closed in, the rainbow would be gone. Little of this has changed. I still believe in the vanishing rainbow and in the dark sky over the mountains. But, with deepening wonder, I also believe in God.

The God I believe in now is different from the God I did not believe in then. It does not intercede, like a royal eagle swooping down from on high, to save the day for those who, outnumbered and outflanked, fight under God's banner. To scale this down, neither is the God I believe in opposed to the Religious Right, nor

bothered in the least by the lack of prayer in public schools. Pray
for rain, and the God I believe in will not answer, whatever the
change in the weather. And it makes no difference who is doing the
praying, for the God I believe in plays no favorites when it comes to
faith or creed. The God I believe in is neither male nor female nor
any divine combination of the two. All this I know, or think I know.
On the other hand, I do not know, and never will know, just what
the God I believe in is. The God I believe in will remain a mystery.
Though hard to put in words, let me share with you my own experience of the mystery of God.

My faith is grounded on two principles, humility and openness.
As to the first of these—and it may be a truism—the more I know of
life, death, and God, the greater my ignorance appears. Beyond
every ridge lies another slope. Beyond every promontory looms yet
another vast and awesome range. While cursed (or blessed) with
the knowledge of our own mortality, however far we trek, we shall
never know the answers to questions like "Why?" or "What does
life mean?" For this reason, I cannot embrace a rigidly dogmatic
faith. I could not do so even should the dogma be fashioned wholly
according to my own test of unfolding truth and time.

This is the lesson humility teaches. Alone, such wisdom is insufficient, reminding us only of what we cannot hope to know.
On the other hand, openness (the possibility principle) invites
us to probe life as deeply as we can, without regard to limits. As
Wayne Rood told me once, "Theology is the art of saying a little
more than one knows." Accepting these limits, while remaining
open to explore as fully as possible the unresolvable mystery of our
own and our shared being, we grow both intellectually and spiritu-
ally. The mystery of life becomes ever deeper and more wondrous,
the gift of life more precious and unaccountable. Remaining open

to the unknown, we enter further into it. We grow in knowledge, yes, and in ignorance, but also in wonder and, finally, in trust.

My own forays are usually journeys taken in meditation or prayer, but they may also come through music, art, literature, nature, or some magical moment of human interaction. Losing myself, I find myself, and my perspective is changed. I can describe the experience only as one of mystical union in that which is greater than all of its parts and yet present in each, in that which gives meaning to all, beyond explanation, beyond knowing or naming.

Such experiences lead me back, not always but often, to God. Again, God is not God's name. God is our name for the mystery that dwells within and looms beyond the limits of our being. Life force, spirit, ground of being, these too are names for the unnameable that I am now, together with so many other seekers, content to call my God.

When I pray to God, the answer comes from within, not to the specifics of my prayer, but in response to my hunger for meaning and peace. God's answer is not a what or a how, not a when or a why, but a YES. *Choose life and trust life. Grow in service and love. Take nothing for granted. Be thankful for the gift. Suffer well. Dare to risk much. Consecrate your world with laughter and with tears. Know not what I am or who I am or how I am, only that I am with you.* This is God's answer to my prayers.

As I plunge deeper, in fits and starts, seeking to penetrate the mystery of life and God, the mystery grows. It grows in wonder, power, moment, and depth. There are times, many times, when God is not with me, times of distraction, fragmentation, alienation, and brokenness. But when I open myself to God, incrementally my wholeness is restored. Perhaps that which I call God is no more than the mystery of life itself. I cannot know, nor do I care, for the power that emanates from deep within the heart of this mystery is redemptive. It is divine. Without hoping or presuming to understand it, opening myself to it, I find peace.

God will remain mysterious. That is as it should be. Anything less would do no justice to the wonders of consciousness, love and pain, life and death. Responding to these miracles, responding to God's YES, I can do no other than to answer "Yes" in return.

"Yes, I place my trust in Thee. Yes, I offer up my heartfelt thanks."

8. Poetry in Motion

A monk is a bird who flies very fast without knowing where he is going. And always arrives where he went, in peace without knowing where he comes from.

—*Thomas Merton,*

NEW SEEDS OF CONTEMPLATION

Living is a form of not being sure, not knowing what is next or how. The moment you know how, you begin to die a little. The artist never entirely knows. We guess. We may be wrong, but we take leap after leap in the dark. —*Agnes de Mille*

Is Shakespeare right? Is all the world a stage, with all the men and women merely players? Not exactly. Remember, we help write the play in which we are featured. This is a challenge, because we don't control our own material. The curtain may fall before we have a chance to perform our monologue or sing our swan song. On the other hand, we needn't follow the script. We can improvise, try out lines, strike poses, experiment while discovering, as best we can, what the play in which we're featured is about.

With minor credits as co-author, and if we are fortunate, able to perform in four or five acts, we play critic and reviewer as well. All the more intriguing, we are also in the audience. The question is, would you see the play again? And how would you rate your performance? Two stars, three stars? Did it make you cry? I hope so. Did it make you laugh? If it did, add another star.

[107]

How about the rest of the audience, your co-critics, co-authors, and co-performers? This play has been running almost forever, you know. Fortunately, we can review earlier performances and judge our own accordingly. But I can assure you of this. The most important critics are our fellow actors, those who share the stage with us.

Think about the stage. We are entering another millennium. A thousand years is a significant span of time. Few of us can trace our own genealogies even a third that far back. To pique the millennial lust, since our calendar is predicated on a monk's calculation of the birth of Jesus, every manner of apocalyptic musing attended the latest turning of the millennial clock. Jesus was not born two thousand years ago, by the way. According to the latest scholarship, Jesus Christ was born four years Before Christ. The promised and long-awaited end times came and passed several years ago.

Millenarianism is an archly rational notion. It computes numbers until it finds meaning in them. Also, understandably but undeniably, it is a narcissistic notion. Given how many people have lived and died before us (some seven dead for every one alive today), how privileged we are to be among the select few actually to be present for Armageddon. So let me expand the millennial frame from Western Christian time not to Cosmic time—something far too forbidding even to contemplate—but to earth time. Looking at ourselves in terms of earth time serves both the cause of humility (a reminder that everything does not pivot, or teeter-totter on our own little fulcrum of history) and the possibility of awe (the "wow," or "isn't that amazing" that puts everything else in perspective).

Not so very long ago, about half a century, biologist H. J. Muller sketched an earth-based time line. One of my congregants adapted this for my amusement. I certainly was amused, but also humbled and awestruck. It is the perfect antidote to millennial madness. (I came to All Souls Church directly upon completing my doctorate at Harvard; hence the details of her conceit.)

Picture this in your mind. From the beginning of time until now, life on earth is connected on a string leading from Cambridge, Massachusetts, to New York City, from Harvard's Widener Library to the pulpit of All Souls. We're talking some 3 or 4 billion years, plotted on a time line that runs a couple of hundred miles, or about 250 years to an inch.

Start out in Cambridge on the library steps, with the ur-paramecium, the first primeval protoplasm. And then fast-forward. Skip the rest of Massachusetts, Rhode Island, and Connecticut. In fact, skip everything from Harvard Yard to Yankee Stadium. In the infield, somewhere between second base and the pitcher's mound, the first amphibians finally emerge from the creative caldron of waters. Not until we get to Harlem do birds and mammals appear, little flying creatures and then furry land dwellers that give birth live and suckle their young. For a time these coexist with dinosaurs, who enter the picture in mid-Harlem and disappear by about 125th Street. Monkeys show up on 96th Street. That's a long way from Cambridge. But in human terms, it's also a far stretch from All Souls Church, for even when we get to the front steps at 80th and Lexington, the cleverest creature we will encounter is a chimpanzee.

I invite you to enter the sanctuary. As you do, you will be greeted by a Neanderthal—your usher—perhaps no more an ancestor than the chimp, but more co-pathetic, larger, slightly less hairy, somehow more familiar. Now walk the aisle. The whole aisle. Not until the first pew does our own species, *Homo sapiens,* show up. As an aside, this is perhaps the first and last time that any human has chosen to sit in the foremost pew of what we might perceive as an empty church. As for the great storied history of humankind, in unrecorded yet slightly remembered form (some 14,000 years ago), civilization begins at the bottom of the chancel steps.

Twenty minutes from now you will be finishing this book. I am standing on the top step delivering my benediction. Here's what happens in an almost unimaginably short span of time. (If we were dealing in words rather than miles, with page one representing the beginning of life on this planet, everything I am about to recount would take place during the period that follows the last word of this book). King Tut is on the lip of the next-to-the-top step. Two inches from my toe, Europeans discover America, and Copernicus discovers—at the time a heretical notion—that the sun does not circle the earth. One inch away is the Declaration of Independence; half an inch away, Darwin's theory of evolution, in many quarters still a heresy; a third of an inch away, we witness the invention of the airplane. As for that microbe on the edge of my shoe (not my shoe, of course, the shoe of the future), that microbe might actually be Bill Gates.

With respect to the millennium, between my toe and Cambridge, the second millennium Christian standard time is also on the top step. So was the millennium before that, back to the very birth of Jesus. With 250 years to an inch, two thousand years take up little more than half a step. Reverse your steps from here all the way back to Cambridge and march forward. Or wind your clock back twenty-four hours and wait till the last second passes. Or read the last of 4 million entries in the Los Angeles White Pages. In the saga of life, that is when all human history took place.

I hope you feel humble now. Not humiliated. Humiliation is what people do to one another, people who feel smarter, more knowledgeable, or more pious than the person they believe themselves so fully entitled to humiliate. Humble is without pretense or airs, not

"I'm weak and you are strong," but "we know so little; we are truly one."

Whatever apocalyptic seers imagine they can divine as they dust the final step on the long journey from Cambridge to All Souls for eternal fingerprints strikes me as comparatively uninteresting. Far more interesting is the entire journey, the pageant of creation, not humans playing scales but humans together scaling mountains.

Is this a theology? For me it is. Despite all the climactic and evolutionary toing and froing, that we have managed to emerge over eons from the swamp and done such remarkable things in so short a time is nothing less than amazing. It is beyond belief that one step of millions from the beginning of life until now carries the burden and weight of human history, philosophy, theology, science, art, music, and poetry. As biologist Ursula Goodenough writes, "The Epic of Evolution is our warp, destined to endure, commanding our universal gratitude and reverence and commitment. And then, after that, we are all free to be artists, to render in language and painting and song and dance our ultimate hopes and concerns and understandings of human nature."

When Copernicus discovered that we are not the center of the universe, we were made not weaker but stronger. If we may happen to be less central to the scheme of things than we once imagined, we discovered this ourselves. We may be dwarfed by the immensities of space, but the mind that measures these immensities manifests its own greatness. Halfway in size between the cosmos and the smallest particle of creation, we exist in a kind of equipoise, our DNA as amazing as the number of our personal stars. As Nicholas Wade points out in an article on cells, "The nucleus of a human cell holds more than six feet of DNA, containing all a person's genes. . . . If it were possible to align all the DNA strands of a baby in a single line, it would be long enough to make, on average, 15 round trips from the sun to Pluto, the farthest planet in the solar system." I don't begin to understand this, but it reminds me that we are neither less nor more incredible than the universe we ponder.

Contrast such evidence with the triumphalist Christian, Muslim, or Orthodox Jewish theologians who claim that the entire universe exists for and in some strange way because of us. To them we are the object of all the orbs, all the hundred billion galaxies. Not only that, but even now God is preparing to drop the curtain, having chosen a particular year on a particular planet in a particular solar system in a particular galaxy as the stage where all creation will be redeemed. Recent-day true believers might take a page from ortho-dox theologian and gadfly G. K. Chesterton, who described his own generation as "the small and arrogant oligarchy of those who merely happen to be walking about."

I'm embarrassed to repeat this, but he did say it, though he re-tracted it later, and what he said could not more starkly differen-tiate my theology from his. As the millennium approached, the Reverend Jerry Falwell said that it is self-evident (1) that the Anti-christ is alive today, and (2) that he is a Jewish man. Dr. Falwell appears to know ever so much more than I could ever presume to imagine knowing. On the other hand, I can see him clearly, right next to Bill Gates, a microbe on the edge, not of my shoe of course (I am a microbe too), simply on the edge of the next tiny foot, liter-ally millions of feet from the first foot, from the first tiny step of mil-lions of steps from the beginning of life until now.

We both respond to the creation with awe. The difference is this: Jerry Falwell and so many others find it awesome that eight inches ago something happened guaranteeing that eight inches later the world would end. I find it awesome that more than two hundred miles ago something happened that permits us, so many miles later, to ponder the mystery and majesty of the cosmos. Jerry Falwell is no less religious than I am, but contrasting his fixation on eight inches of history with my celebration of two hundred miles, the difference between our theological approaches could not be more manifest.

To me, the creation is poetry in motion, an ultimately unfathomable and still unfolding masterpiece. We are part of what we ponder, part of the poetry we recite, scan, and interpret. You may interpret it one way, Jerry Falwell a second, and I a third. That's fine. That's the way the poetry of God works. It admits to many interpretations, but each warrants a degree of humility. Ultimately the only real difference between us is this: though no less ignorant of what life means, those of us with a two-hundred-mile parallax vision are more aware of our ignorance than are those—equally ignorant—with eight-inch blinders. This said, what we have in common is far greater than anything that may divide us. All of us— for one another's sake—need to remember this. As Diane Winston, a fellow of the Center for the Study of American Religion at Princeton University, writes, "Different traditions are different—and it is good they remain so. But at best, they offer a vision and a means of common purpose. The question besetting the next millennium is how to live with and learn from people who look, believe and behave differently than we do."

Here is my favorite etymology. Think of how intimately these words relate: human, humane, humanitarian, humor, humble, humility, humus. Dust to dust. But also heart to heart, laugh to laugh, and life to life. To be fully human is not to know the answers to unanswerable questions. It is to be humane, humble, gifted with a sense of humor, and mindful that truly we are one.

You may have wondered about the feather. In Egyptian mythology, when we die our life is weighed on balance to determine whether we sail across the heavenly waters or instead die again, this time forever. The ancient Egyptians believed that the heart was the organ of intelligence and memory. Upon our death, Anubis, the god of embalming, would place our heart in the scales, weighing it for sins. He weighed it against a feather. If our heart was lighter than a feather, we passed the test. If it was heavier than a feather, we didn't. The feather was a symbol of Ma'at, the goddess of truth and order. Think of feathers also as a symbol for the beauty and lightness of being. As G. K. Chesterton wrote, "Angels can fly because they take themselves lightly." Feathers help both angels and tiny birds to soar. And then, one by one, feathers flutter gracefully to the ground. If we take our lives lightly and the world seriously, pursuing our projects with both gentleness and strength, we have nothing to fear when the final reckoning comes. As Emily Dickinson said, "Hope is the thing with feathers."

Let me leave you with three things that invest my own life with meaning.

Enthusiasm: being filled with God
Ecstasy: standing outside of myself
Empathy: being within another

For the discovery and creation of meaning, enthusiasm (being divinely inspired) is an elixir. Enthusiasm is passion. God invades its etymology, but for meaning to be found, the object of our passions need not always be noble. I am a Lyle Lovett enthusiast, a New York Met enthusiast, a crossword puzzle enthusiast, a photography enthusiast. To get enthusiastic about a basketball tournament, a new diet, or a favorite hobby is a wonderful thing. These too are projects. They fill us with energy and unite us with others who share our enthusiasms.

Of course, not all meanings are equal. When our enthusiasms drift out of balance (an enthusiasm for play distracting us from work, or for work estranging us from family), when we intently devote ourselves to some project in our life not worthy of intense devotion, the "god within us" becomes an idol. But, when we approach our most important projects with passion, we likely will sustain them and, therefore, evoke from them a sense of meaning. If so, with our vitality thus enhanced, God may indeed dwell within us.

The second word is *ecstasy*. This seems a selfish word. It is not. Ecstasy means to stand outside of oneself. When we stand outside ourselves, we connect with something larger and more all-embracing. In Jesus' words, we experience ecstasy when we lose ourselves and thereby find ourselves, when we give away our life and discover a greater life, one we are a part of, not apart from. We can lose ourselves in lovemaking, in music, in a book, in prayer. To lose ourselves in something other than ourselves is ecstasy. As with enthusiasm, ecstasy too can imbue each of our projects with added meaning. Whatever our endeavor, any time we place our concerns and worries aside, any time we enter into a larger life, we open ourselves to the possibility of an ecstatic encounter. Since it is impossible to experience ecstasy while lost in self-absorption, ecstasy liberates us from the one thing least conducive to the art of meaning. To practice lifecraft well, you must stand outside yourself. Until you do, you cannot connect with others, and connecting with others is what meaning is about.

My third word is *empathy:* to be within another and feel another's pain or joy. When two people become one, both are enhanced, as is the meaning in their lives. One reason I love the ministry so deeply is that those of us who serve in it have daily opportunities for empathy. We don't always seize them. The finest minister often fails to rise to the occasions that life and death offer. I speak from experience. Many people have a more developed gift for intimacy than I do. But I am blessed with so many opportunities. When I seize one, forgetting myself and entering another's life, I never fail to learn a little more about my own life's meaning.

When I am with someone who is dying, I feel my own death. I connect with what it means to be alive and then to die. If you are in pain because of a failure or loss, even if you are celebrating some accomplishment, invite another to suffer or celebrate with you. For the discovery and creation of meaning, nothing is more important. You can examine your life all you wish, but you won't begin to sense life's meaning until you connect with others, feel their pain as if it were your own, and also share their joy.

One more thing you should try to keep in mind. We are all going to die. This is not an unmixed tragedy. If you could love forever, work and play forever, neither love, work, nor play would be nearly as charged with meaning as they are by the fact that each will end.

A drowning man sees his entire life pass before his eyes. How long does this take? About a minute. Take the next minute of your life. You are drowning. You are about to die. No more options. No more projects. One minute is all you have left. Your entire life is about to pass before your eyes. Close them. What do you see?

A minute is quite a long time. Had you been ready, you might have been able to fill it more thoughtfully. But that's the way death works. We hit a trap door. It opens, and we fall. We may fall for a minute, a month, or a year, but once the trapdoor springs, there is nothing we can do. Even more sadly, nothing will change all the minutes, hours, days, weeks, months, and years that slipped by unconsciously before we fell. At their dying moment, no one wishes that they had spent more time in the office, made more money, read more books, or become a better squash player.

So what gives our lives meaning? Here is my short list. Kindness does. Also forgiveness. Generosity. Enthusiasm. Ecstasy. Empathy. Above all love, given and received. For any of these things, one minute is not a bad start. If you spend most of those that remain to you in ways you will blessedly forget during the minute before you die, forgive yourself. But invest at least a few in saving your life before you lose it. Finish a good project. Start a new one. Ponder the cosmos. Shake your head in wonder. Tell someone you love them. Kindness never hurts.

Does life have meaning? Yes, life has meaning, more meaning than any of us will ever know.

Afterword

Bidding you farewell, I offer this final invitation. Think of your life as a book, difficult but potentially worthy. The cover attracted you. The first few chapters won your interest. Not a great book perhaps, but a good book. How will it turn out?

Thumbing through the pages of our lives, sometimes we get stuck. We read a single page over and over. Surely, this has happened to you. Often it happens to me. I read a page only to realize that my mind wasn't tracking. So I go back to the top to read it again. As often as not, when I reread the page, I get even less out of it than I did the first time. I concentrate harder, but to no avail. I read sentence after sentence, and then, on the bottom of the page, realize I still haven't caught the drift. So I go back to the top again, more anxious and dedicated than before to make sense of what I am reading. This time I really concentrate. I read the passage word by word. The words ring in my brain, but now they don't even compose sentences. The harder I try to get through this page of my book, the more incomprehensible it becomes. It means absolutely nothing.

Afterword

If you are stuck at some point in your life, when the harder you try the less you comprehend, when you have read the same page three times with diminishing returns, my suggestion is this: Turn the page.

You will miss something. I understand that. Sometimes trying to find something you know you have missed delays you from discovering things that await you when you turn the page. Action. New characters. A turn in plot. Or the development of character, which almost never happens when we are stuck, going over the same old page, caught in a trance, looking for paragraphs and finding only sentences, or for sentences and finding only words.

How many ruts there are. How often we go back over what our parents did to us. Or some lover or hater, a bad boss, bad gene, or bad friend, even our own bad decisions indelibly etched on the page, forever to haunt us as we read them again and again, waiting for some new insight, afraid to turn the page. Turn the page.

Don't assume that you have to get everything right with the past and the present before you dare approach an unknown future. Don't focus so hard that your focus blurs and the images double—twice the problems, twice the troubles. You've been there. I know you have. It has to make sense and you just can't make sense of it, so you read it again and again. Resist the temptation. Turn the page. Put yourself in the big picture. Look out, not in. Look up. Try the heavens. Try a star, one of your twenty-five (or 2.5 trillion) stars. Try a loved one. Connect. Try enthusiasm, ecstasy, empathy. Try the God project. Try praying. Practice dying. Then live. If you are stuck in one passage of your life, restock and relaunch. Take your lifecraft out of drydock. Turn the page.

I based my last book on the wisdom of Ecclesiastes—"for everything there is a season, and a time for every purpose under heaven."

Afterword

Let me close this one by quoting from one of my favorite folksing-ers, Pete Seeger. He added just one word to the preacher's wisdom, repeating it for good measure.

"To everything—turn, turn, turn—there is a season—turn, turn, turn."

Trust this.

Turn the page.